Essay:

Modern Arnis

Personal Insights

On The Art of Remy Presas

Prof. Dan Anderson

Essays On

Modern Arnis

Personal Insights on the Art of Remy Presas

Published in the United States by DAMA Books & Videos.

This book is dedicated to the memory of Remy Presas.
May his smile continue to infect us all.

PRINTED IN THE UNITED STATES
First Edition November 2022

Contact Dan Anderson @ www.superdanonlinelibrary.com

Table Of Contents

David Fogge Interview continued

Remy Amador Presas

(December 19, 1936 – August 28, 2001)

Introduction

I first met Remy Presas in 1979 or 1980 at a tournament in Oakland, California. He was with Fred King and me. I've told the story many times about how I tried to blow him off but failed. When he did a hands-on demonstration of what he could do, the top of my head blew off. I had not only felt the touch of a bonafide master but I had my first experience of where I was going to next in my martial arts journey. By the way, I do include that full story later in this text so I won't leave you in a mystery. Besides, it's a funny one.

The back story here is that at the time I was a tournament karate champion. I had been in the Top Ten rated fighters for around four years by that time and in the words of Tom Callos, was in the upper 2% of all-time karate fighters. I was young, athletic, and had a very inquiring mind. But I was also nearing the end of my interest in the game. In the back of my mind was the question, *"Where do I go from here?"* I didn't want to be a former champion attempting to live through my glory years. I wanted to continue and progress but hadn't seen the route yet. That afternoon in Oakland changed everything.

I have now been immersed in Modern Arnis and Filipino martial arts for over 40 years. The fascination with it never ceases. What initially amazed me was how easily Prof. Remy could disarm me. I had the stick in my hand and then all of a sudden, he had my stick. He was so smooth and commanding. From there, it was the flow of motion.

I have studied the principal concepts and actions of many different martial arts. Like I said, I have an intensely inquiring mind. I have always been interested in internal martial arts, especially baguazhang. The concept of relaxed application has always fascinated me. Well, you couldn't get a whole lot more relaxed than Prof. Remy.

Again, fascinating.

I was his student and he was my sole teacher for 21 years. I studied no other FMA than Modern Arnis until after his passing. I made an interesting breakthrough in the 1980s. Prof. Remy was going through a period of ill health and I was wondering what I would do if he died. I stopped listening to him and began to really observe and *feel* him. This began my quantum jump in skill and understanding of his art.

Mind you, I was already tracking with him on a technical basis. I already had 14 years of world class skills and experience before I met him. I picked up his techniques so quickly that Fred King said to me one time, *"You must learn this by osmosis."* Loren Christensen, my first karate teacher, wrote in a book review that I was a "natural learner." I didn't miss a thing. Every seminar I came home with notes and drawings of what he'd taught that time. I'd bring them to the class I taught in my school and we drilled them thoroughly. I never went to a seminar wondering if I'd missed anything. Nope. Between my own skill-sets and personal powers of observation backed up by my understanding of martial theory, I never missed a beat.

Back to the quantum jump. I began comparing what I observed and felt when he did applications on me to the principles of martial arts that I had studied. Let me make a clarification here. The author/karate practitioner Kenji Tokitsu made an interesting distinction one time. He said he'd studied 50+ styles of karate. Then he said that there is a difference between studying and training in an art. He had only *trained* in a couple of karate styles but had *studied* the differences and similarities in others. This is exactly what I did. I studied the heck out of everything I could get my hands on but only trained in, at first, karate and later Modern Arnis. I did train in baguazhang for a short time later on.

What I felt when Prof. Remy did applications on me was the relaxed firmness of how taiji and bagua are supposed to be applied. Firm, yet lacking in tension. Strong, yet not strong-arming. Fluid, but not wimpy. I didn't know it in 1980 but this is what I was looking for.

My quantum jump was in my research in replicating Prof. Remy's ease of application. I was not going to attempt to mirror his physical actions because we had different body types and personal degrees of understanding. But ease of application? That I could do.

Then it was how to communicate it. Prof. Remy was terrific at empowerment. He was not so good at communicating his art in a way that was easily understood. English was his second language and he didn't have a scientific mind. That's okay. That's where I come in. Since his passing I have produced ~20 books and numerous DVDs on the subject. This is my payback to the man who selflessly gave me his art.

Oh, something to mention. What has Modern Arnis given to me? Longevity in the martial arts. The essence of Modern Arnis, the Flow, has enabled me to continue moving smoothly as I approach my seventh decade (70 years old in November 2022). I am not a broken down old karate man who hobbles around. Far from it. My movements remain supple and relaxed. That was his gift to me. Thank you, sir.

Modern Arnis – A Thumbnail Sketch
Modern Arnis is the brainchild of Remy Presas. One of the fascinating things about the art is that there are only one or two times Prof. Remy, himself, defined Modern Arnis. One time was in an interview in Karate International Magazine, May/June issue 1989. The exchange is printed here verbatim:

> KIM - "What is the difference between Modern Arnis and regular Arnis?"
> RP – "Well, it is like in America, because you had mathematics today you have modern mathematics. Modern Arnis is more practical, easier and flexible. That is why it is called Modern Arnis. There is a system. There are rules to follow like today of modern English and modern mathematics. It is a simplified system that teachers know how to use both the stick or the same techniques empty handed. It is a very effective martial arts system."

Pretty much every other definition came from the writers of articles about Prof. Remy or Modern Arnis. For me, Modern Arnis is a Filipino art of self-defense that entails the use of single stick, double stick, stick and dagger, empty hand techniques, and anyos (forms).

Prof. Remy's history is thoroughly covered in a previous book of mine, *Modern Arnis – The Martial Art of Remy Presas**. The bare bones facts are:

- Young Remy began training with his grandfather, Leon, when he was around 6 years old.
- He left Hinigaran at age 14 and began training in balintawak eskrima with Rodolfo Mongcol. He graduated from Mongcol to Timoteo Maranga and finally to the founder of balintawak, Anciong Bacon.
- He stayed with balintawak for roughly 7 years and then went back to his home town and started a school.
- He relocated to Manila and taught in the school system.
- He visited the United States in 1974 and due to political reasons, he returned in 1975.
- In 1980 he stormed the US seminar scene virtually recreating it and continued to do so until he fell ill in 2000.
- He retired from teaching and passed away in August 2001.

Here are several of his career highlights.
- 1982 Black Belt Magazine Hall of Fame Instructor of the Year. This was huge. It really pointed out how impact he had on the United States.
- 1994 Black belt Magazine Hall of Fame Weapons Expert of the Year.
- Magazine articles include Fighting Stars December 1974, Black Belt magazine September 1981, Black Belt magazine August 1982, Black Belt magazine yearbook 1982, Karate International magazine May/June 1989, Inside Kung Fu December 1990, Black Belt magazine Yearbook 1994, Black Belt magazine August 1998, Martial Arts Illustrated October 1998.
- He wrote the book *Modern Arnis The Filipino Art of Stick Fighting*, published by Ohara Publications.

*Modern Arnis - The Martial Art of Remy Presas - www.superdanonlinelibrary.com

Essays

This first section is a series of various essays I posted up on Facebook. I have gotten many, many good responses from the readers so I decided to put them into one collection.

Why Do I Write So Much About Modern Arnis?

Here I am, Super Dan, known across the planet as a world class karate guy doing the bulk of my writing and videoing about Modern Arnis. What's up with this, anyway? There are several reasons.

The first of them is that this is a transformative art for me. The teaching of Remy Presas was the bridge between me being a karate jock and a martial artist. As far as my personal history goes, this is huge. Huge. Modern Arnis contained everything I had read about in martial arts but was lacking in my karate training. You might say that my karate training was limited…and you'd be right. I had the stand-up striking arts down pat. Hell, I was a four time national champion when I met Prof. Remy yet my art was strikingly (pun intended) incomplete. I was a karate boy, through and through. That all changed with Modern Arnis.

Something that is that transformational is worth writing and videoing about.

Second is that there is very little material out there that really dissects the physical training in the art. This is my bread and butter. Let me back up a bit. In 1980 American Freestyle Karate – A Guide To Sparring was published. This was the first book that went beyond the primer stage of the books at the time. It was the first in depth book on the subject. I poured my heart and soul into that book and it was a critical success. This book became required reading for belt rank in many karate schools across the country. It was that good.

Remy Presas published three books and a number of videos on Modern Arnis. They were great examples of what he could do but, in my opinion only the really experienced eye could take what he was doing and translate it down for the "common man." Translating martial motion for consumption for the common man is my cup of tea. I love translating the rich variety of Modern Arnis into easily understandable concepts and applications in both my books and videos.

 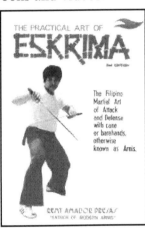 

One thing about books – they have a permanency of sorts. Books have been around in some form or another for millennia and will be around for more. People have written on papyrus, scrolls, and finally gotten writings into print. Print will stick with us despite the being in the electronic age.

One thing about me is that I am not afraid of the printed word. I am neither illiterate nor dyslexic. Also, for some reason I have a knack for communicating concepts and techniques so that they are easily understood the book and video buyers end. I look at this way – Did you buy my product so that you can be confused? I'll bet not. My purpose is to illuminate, not to confuse.

In one way I consider myself an archivist. I want to present and preserve the art. Today with the ease of print on demand and home video production tools, my job is that much easier.

Lastly, after over 56 years and four tenth dan certificates under my belt, why am I so in love with this art? The Flow. Prof. Remy stressed to me the importance of the Flow in Modern Arnis. It is the Flow that has helped preserve my body. Mish Handwerker told me of meeting up with Bruce Chiu at a seminar camp they both taught at. Mish was teaching Ryukyu Kempo while Bruce was teaching Modern Arnis. Mish recalled to me talking with Bruce and Bruce saying, *"I finally met Dan. He is almost 70 years old and he is really GOOD!"*

Why can I move with fluidity and not be a hobbling old geezer going into my 7th decade? The Flow. With Modern Arnis I transitioned from training in a ballistic based martial art to a smooth motion based one. This has preserved my body.

There is a saying in martial arts regarding belt degrees – *"The first five stripes are for what you get out of the art. The last five stripes are for what you give back."*

Why do I write so much about Modern Arnis? To give back.

Modern Arnis – A Style, System, or a Concept?

Here's another look at Modern Arnis. Well, is it a style? Is it a system? Concept? What the hell is it, anyway? Let's crack open a dictionary and figure it out.

Style - definition:
1. a manner of doing something.
2. a distinctive appearance, typically determined by the principles according to which something is designed.'

Hmmmmm...Modern Arnis a 'style?' Remy Presas had a style but Modern Arnis itself? The practitioners are so varied as to their base arts and roots that this rules out a style. None of us really look like one another in the same manner as perhaps, Cabales Serrada or Kalis Ilustrisimo practitioners. Per the definition above I'd rule out 'style.'

I'll put in here a historical point for you. Where did the term 'style' come from, anyway? From the early practitioners of karate in the US. "Shotokan is my style." Here is the interesting thing. For the early pioneers in the area of karate, English was their second language. When you look at the term 'ryu' as appended to the name of a type of karate such as Goju-ryu, Shito-ryu and so forth, 'ryu' comes from 'ryuha' which means 'school.' It doesn't mean 'style.' "My style" would be more accurately translated as "my school." So, is Modern Arnis a 'style?' Personally, I'd rule that out.

> *System* – definition:
> a set of principles or procedures according to which something is done; an organized framework or method.

Oh, hell no. Especially the use of the words "organized framework or method." The manner in which Prof Remy taught, in the US anyway, was organized chaos. It took the senior students to create methods of teaching others what he taught us. I like to use the term "confetti method" to describe his teaching. He would cover so much in any seminar or camp that it was like someone throwing a fistful of confetti up in the air and whatever stuck to you is what you took home and worked on. 'Organized?' Not on your life!

Set of principles? Prof. Remy was a doer, not a scientific dissector or grad school professor. *"You will do this."* That was about as scientific as he got. That being said, there are a number of the senior students who have organized the materials into an organized progression. The best example I know of is not an American but a German. Dieter Knuttel of the DAV has the most organized Modern Arnis program of any that I have seen. It is very comprehensive. I've had my own program since 1980. There are others as well.

Concept – definition:
an abstract idea; a general notion ('abstract' def: existing in thought or as an idea but not having a physical or concrete existence)

Ahhhhhhhhh, this resonates with me. Prof. Remy left balintawak eskrima in 1957. *"And I told the guy, this Grandmaster, 'If I leave this place, I don't consider me that I am your student anymore but consider me as your friend. You know, but if I leave this place, I will organize my own system, you know, for sport, you know, and for self-defense, not for fighting, for self-defense.' And that's what I did. The guy told me he said, 'Okay, Remy, I think I understand what you mean. You know, you could go and you could organize your own.' You know, because I still use their system. When I change all the, you know, the characteristic[s]. I'm not interested in fighting. I'm interested in education."* *

He already had the germ of an idea of what he wanted to do. He had the concept but nothing worked out yet. He ended up teaching in the public school system. If the public school system in the Philippines is anything like it is in the States, I would bet money that the curriculum was not a comprehensive white – black belt curriculum. It would be a quarter by quarter or semester by semester program. Anyway, it would be a bit organized but not <u>organized</u>. He had the concept of modernizing a fighting and dueling art and making it into, in his exact words, sport, self-defense and education.

This was his abstract notion.

He comes to the United States with Modern Arnis with yet another goal, the promotion of Filipino culture through the teaching of Modern Arnis. My experience with him was that he was promoting the art he loved. He got the concept/slogan "The Art Within Your Art" from Mike Replogle after a seminar. Mike had spotted something that Prof. Remy was doing – showing how Modern Arnis was not some strange thing from another planet but a martial art that had very strong connections with any art you practiced. That was his concept.

*page 19, Modern Arnis - The Martial Art of Remy Presas, www.superdanonlinelibrary.com

This was his abstract notion.

He comes to the United States with Modern Arnis with yet another goal, the promotion of Filipino culture through the teaching of Modern Arnis. My experience with him was that he was promoting the art he loved. He got the concept/slogan "The Art Within Your Art" from Mike Replogle after a seminar. Mike had spotted something that Prof. Remy was doing – showing how Modern Arnis was not some strange thing from another planet but a martial art that had very strong connections with any art you practiced. That was his concept.

I look at Modern Arnis not as a style, system, or a school. I look at it as a concept. You take any of the senior students and you will find differences as well as commonalities. I am planning a seminar in November with the only three Modern Arnis 10th dans in the western hemisphere, Datu Kelly Worden, GM Brian Zawilinski and me. In talking with Kelly, he said it best: *"We all teach different concept from a core art."*

Datu Kelly Worden   GM Brian Zawilinski

I guess that clarifies if there is one pure Modern Arnis or not.
It is not a style. We all have our own styles.
It is not a system yet there are many of us who have systematized it.
It is a concept that continues to live through Prof. Remy's many students worldwide.
Super Dan

Modern Arnis – Combat #1 – Conversation With Chris Chiu

"I don't free-spar. I fight." I remember talking to Chris Chiu about stick sparring one time. I surprised him with that one. He got it when I explained it this way.

Prof. Remy taught principally two things: self-defense and martial art. He taught self-defense moves by the dozen. *"You can do this. You can do this also."* Those of us original gangsters remember hearing that very well. He would go on and on with variation after variation of any one particular technique. My take on it was that there was always an option for any action you did. Your opponent did A. You could do B, C, D, E and F.

Martial art. Let's get into definitions first.
> *Martial*: of or appropriate to war; warlike
> *Art*: something that is created with imagination and skill and that is beautiful or that expresses important ideas or feelings

So, "Martial art" is an aesthetic expression of war or something warlike. Aesthetic war. Boy, is that ever a contradiction of terms! There is nothing beautiful about war or combat. Combat is brutal. Fighting is ugly. Why do you think karate got such a toehold in the Philippines back when Prof. Remy lived there? It was clean and orderly. Everybody did the same thing at the same time (kata and line drills). Everyone wore the same cool pajamas. Everyone followed the rules. This wasn't people getting their bones broken or bodies cut up! This was far more palatable to the general population.

So, when Prof. Remy came to the States, he taught martial ART. And boy did he ever get creative! He threw everything into the kitchen sink into his teaching. Joint locks, disarms, twirling, cane and empty hand forms, classical applications as well as innovations. But he left out one thing – stick FIGHTING.

I came from a karate background and made a pretty good name for myself in the competitive ring during an era when if you messed up, you took your lumps. Get in a time machine and go to Texas sometime. I won there and still took home a number of lumps!

Getting back to my conversation with Chris, I told him there was something missing from Prof. Remy's teaching and that was fighting. Let me give you what I have discovered about fighting:

All fighting is the same. Only the tools and rules of engagement differ.

The same? Even Prof. Remy would say *"It is all the same."* when queried about differences in technique. How is fighting the same? Well, you have principles such as timing, distancing, alignment, structure and so on. You have intangibles such as intent, heart, ability to take a hit and the like. Then you have the type of damage being inflicted on them/you such as the difference between an impact or cutting weapon, a karate or Thai round kick, brass knuckles vs bare fist and so on.

I tell my students that ~97% or arnis is "cool shit" and about 3% is combat. Why? Arnis combat is simple and very unforgiving. You make a mistake and something is broken, pure and simple. I always keep this mind when I do any kind of practice related to combat. When I spar, I don't "spar," not in my mind. In my mind my ass is on the line. I might be playful but I don't play. I watch my range, alignment, timing, and positioning quite acutely.

You might ask "If combat arnis is just 3% of the game why train the other 97%?" Two reasons.

1. Once you get into middle range, that's where all the 97% happens.
2. In the words of Tim Gus, *"There is joy in movement."* I LOVE the martial ART application of arnis. There is an aesthetic joy in the training and playing martial movement. It is this flow of movement that has kept my body supple for this nearly 70 years.

But, I never confuse the two, not for a second. Chris understood what I meant after this explanation.
Super Dan

Modern Arnis – Combat #2 – "Drunken Uncle Frank"

In my previous essay I said that I told my students that 97% of arnis is cool shit and 3% is combat. One week later I still say that. Lol. Let's get onto the subject of empty hands. Oh boy, does Modern Arnis have a ton of empty hand applications. Prof. Remy was as adept without a stick as he was with one. We learned trapping, joint locking, throwing all as part of the overall art. We collected techniques galore.

To me, most all of the applications were what I call "Drunken Uncle Frank moves." Who is Drunken Uncle Frank? He's your mother's favorite brother, a real pain in the butt. He loves to check you out. *"Hey Dan, show me some of that kung fooey shit. Do a move on me...if ya can."* You can't kick him in the groin or poke his eye because he's mom's favorite brother with a drinking problem. *"You know Frankie doesn't mean any harm."* We all know a Drunken Uncle Frank somewhere.

Joint locks, throws, lock flows...Drunken Uncle Frank moves. Why do I say that? Simple. If you try any of these moves on somebody who isn't set up for it, most likely it is going to fail. Yet this is how we are taught the moves. Your partner grabs you. You counter that grab and joint lock them. They tap out. How very civilized. Once in a blue moon it will work without a set up. Here is one example a student of mine, Anita, told me about.

Anita was at a party and she got into some kind of conversation with this guy. He was drunk, turned belligerent and started poking his finger at her. She snagged his finger out of mid-air and pinned him to the ground with a one finger lock until he stopped his shit. It was like out of the movies. This is not an everyday kind of occurrence.

Here's the rub. The moment you make contact with someone, they know something is up. You weren't touching them. Now you are. If they are already in the action of confronting you (how's that for a civilized term?), they already have their attention on you. Very hard to sneak in a joint lock or throw then.

How do you take the 97% of cool shit empty hand moves and turn them into viable combatics? First, know what the move is for. Here is an excerpt from my book on the Modern Arnis anyos (forms), *The North American Legacy of Remy Presas**:

Anyo Functions - Definitions & Purposes
Joint Lock – A joint lock is when you twist the joint farther than it's supposed to go, stretch it farther than it's supposed to go, or straighten it so far that it's goes against the stopping point of the joint. All joint locks hurt. A joint lock has four purposes:
    *To break the joint itself,
    *To move someone from one place to another,
    *To restrain or keep someone from going away, and
    *To throw your opponent to the ground.

A joint lock always has a purpose. A key point for any joint lock is to first set it up with a strike. If you just grab someone and try to execute it, it will most likely not work. Why? Well, the moment you grab someone they know something is up and they will not willingly let you continue.

Prof. Remy & Hock Hockheim

*The North American Legacy of Remy Presas - www.superdanonlinelibrary.com

Throws/Takedowns - A takedown or throw is taking your opponent from a standing position to being on the floor. There are two purposes for a throw or a takedown:

      *To reposition them to the floor so that you can get a head start in getting away from them and

      *To use the impact of the throw to function the same as a strike; to cause your opponent to pause, stop or drop.

Second, you've got to set your opponent up for it. Unfortunately, ever since the jiu-jitsu craze from prior to the WWII days – *"Defeat your attacker with his own strength!"* there has been the myth of effortless application. You touch your opponent and he falls to the ground writhing in pain or is sent flying across the room. Well, in the movies maybe but even Jackie Chan has to break a sweat to do that.

Set up your opponent. In the words of Ron McKinnie, *"Shock before you lock and a blow before you throw."* In other words, hit the sucker and then apply the move. You may have to hit the sucker more than once. All well and good.

Then you can do the cool shit.

Unless it's Drunken Uncle Frank, mom's favorite brother. Then you're on your own, mate.
Super Dan

The Spirit of Modern Arnis

I got back from Connecticut Modern Arnis Camp hosted by Brian Zawilinski and it was filled with the spirit of Modern Arnis. I got to thinking *"What is the spirit of Modern Arnis anyway?"* A martial art, in and of itself, is just a martial art. It is a curriculum or style or system or concept (more on that in later post). A martial art is not a spirit and doesn't inherently contain any spirit.

So, what is the spirit of Modern Arnis? I believe the spirit resides in the founder and then is handed down to the students. So, when I look at the spirit of Modern Arnis, I look at how Remy Presas presented the art. That really defines it for me.

- Prof. Remy was generous with this teaching, not stingy.
- He was electric, not dull or apathetic.
- He was inclusive, not exclusive.
- He was empowering, not demeaning.
- He was fun, not Sgt. Presas of the Marine Corps.
- He was progressive, not stuck in the past or regressive.
- And we must include how freakin' skilled he was.

These attributes of Prof. Remy say it all for me and these are the attributes that I strive for in myself. These are the attributes I look for in others to see if they have the "Spirit of Modern Arnis."

The instructors at Connecticut Camp; Brian Zawilinski, Chad Bailey, Roland Rivera and me (I feel) I have it. Other instructors like Kelly Worden, Bruce Chiu, Bram Frank, Michael Bates, Dieter Knuttel have it as well. We were all students of the late Prof. Presas and we work on passing it down. Not just the art but the spirit he had when teaching us. And each of us being separate and distinct personalities, we do not mimic the Professor but instead, bring our own personalities into our instructional methods while maintaining the attributes of the spirit.

I could go on and on and on but I think you got the point. The founder passed over 20 years ago but the spirit continues on.
Super Dan

What Is Meant By "The Art Within Your Art"?

When Remy Presas first came to the US, he had nothing but arnis to earn a living by. Remy, with his life in danger, hurriedly left The Philippines in 1975 and everything he had there. He had an operating school, a good position in the educational system, a family. He lost it all – the works. His friend, Dean Stockwell (below left), wanted to get him into the movies but that wasn't his goal.

He had done some teaching in the States on his previous visit in the San Francisco area but he hardly had the following he would later enjoy. He had nothing but his love for arnis and the drive to survive. He was just plugging along and then came the explosion.

I was there during the "explosion" of Modern Arnis in the States and have a good historical perspective on it. I met Remy Presas in 1979 and took my first seminar in 1980. It was electric. The slogan *The Art Within Your Art* was not yet a thing. We did Modern Arnis and he trained us hard. I can still clearly remember the group doing a combination umbrella/slanting defensive drill and him yelling *"Harder! Faster!"* Interspersed with the stick work were empty hand applications. We would go back and forth between the two, amassing lumps, bruises, and lots of smiles. Especially lots of smiles.

The first broad public use of *The Art Within Your Art* came from a *Black Belt* magazine article in the August 1980 issue. Brainerd Kebbelman titled the article, "Arnis – The Art Within Your Art." How did the term come about? I got in contact with Mike Replogle, who ran a school in

17

Los Angeles and was an OG in the 1980s who was also featured in that article and asked him about it. Here is some history for you.

> Mike Replogle: *"Yes... that was me. I came up with the phrase as a tag line for the Black Belt article; then it became the title. Working with Remy and doing seminars, I was seeing how the stick is a link that connected different styles (a take-off on the earlier "link between divided arts" article with Jeff Arnold), and I had students from Aikido to Kung fu and Karate and the "The Art Within You Art" came to me when we were talking about doing another article.*
>
> *"I was doing a lot of Arnis and other magazine articles at that time and although I came up with the idea for the article, I didn't write that one. And yes, the phrase was not ever used before that, but it was pretty catchy, Remy liked it and it was great for marketing, so I'm not surprised that it caught on."*

The fascinating thing is that nowhere in that article does Remy Presas use that phrasing. Here are some quotes from that article. After telling how the signature empty hand move of arnis, the parry-grab-strike, is done, Presas goes on to say this. *"So if you know the high inside block and back fist of karate, you know something of arnis."* He also says earlier in the article, *"Those who understand arnis cannot say anything bad about other arts, because they know arnis contains aspects and*

Mike Replogle

elements of all these other arts." And the last quote in the article says it all. "It all comes back to the flow. By developing the ability to flow the student is gaining the ability to experiment. He will find out what works for him. I show the student many steps, how arnis is a part of the other arts."

What Prof. Remy was doing was showing the student how to make the connection with whatever art he or she was training in, how arnis was both exotic yet something they "already knew." Why was making this connection important? Here is where living through an important time of martial arts history comes into play.

Prior to Remy Presas teaching Modern Arnis, nobody cross-trained as far as seminars went. Karate people went to karate seminars, judo people went to judo seminars, and so on. I should say hardly anybody instead of nobody cross-trained but that was the nature of things. Remember, there was no internet then, no YouTube or Facebook, nothing like that. Instant communication and instant access was, at best, a long distance phone call. Martial artists stayed within their own realms...until Remy came along. His enthusiasm and ability to "connect the dots" was something unheard of up to then.

When he taught Modern Arnis, he taught it in such a manner that the student could make sense of a number of things in the art they trained in yet perform it in an arnis manner. Karate people could do it. Taekwondo people could do it. Kenpo people could do it. Anybody could do it. Fred King said in the referenced article: *"More than just about anybody I've seen, Professor Presas has an ability to transfer his own expertise in the art of arnis to his students. It's almost like a transfusion."* Remy was inclusive, not exclusive.

So, what is *The Art Within Your Art*? It is how Modern Arnis had so much more in common with what you already do.

It is the personification of something Prof. Remy said all the time – *"It is all the same."* Yep. It IS all the same. That is the art within your art.
Super Dan

Understanding Modern Arnis – Rocky Pasiwk
(These next two essays were not written by me but were contributions to my book *Modern Arnis – The Martial Art of Remy Presas*. I feel they are perfect for this one. This first essay was written by a pre-1980 student of Prof. Remy, Rocky Pasiwk. Read on.)

I often ruffle many a feather when I talk to people about modern arnis and explain to them just exactly what the art was, especially when first taught here in America. Modern Arnis was taught by GM Remy Presas as the "Filipino Art of Self Defense." Yep, reread that, "The Filipino Art of Self Defense."

His intentions were to spread part of the Filipino culture through-out America and the world. This could not be possible teaching "stick fighting." He was so far ahead of all other masters of his time. Serrada was here in America decades before Remy, as were, a number of systems of Kali, the Lastra Bothers, even Inosanto blend. Yet in a few short years Modern Arnis outgrew all of them. It did this not because it was a better art, not by far. In an actual stick fight back in the 70s and 80s very few Modern Arnis guys could stand for more than a few seconds in front of a PTK (Pikiti Tersia) guy or any of a number of other systems.

But it didn't matter. That's not what Modern Arnis was for. It was a form of self-defense, designed to blend with any other art. It wasn't an art that said, "Hey, we are better than your taekwondo so quit learning that crap and train with us." No. Modern Arnis was an art that said, "Hey, what you do is cool and you could add some of our stuff to make it even cooler, our stick and knife techniques can flow with your techniques. Our art is 'THE ART WITHIN YOUR ART.' We only want to help make you better while you help make us better."

For the most part, Remy didn't like the idea of people leaving a seminar sore in any way, shape or form. He wanted you to leave feeling like you learned so much that it was going to take you months to figure it all out, but you would and you would add your flavor to it. This I'm sure will upset some people, but there was a reason why other Grand Masters would do seminars and have 10, 15, maybe 20 people show up Remy would have 50, 60 even 70 people show up.

I remember going to seminars of other GMs. We spent hours on delivering the first two strikes with proper footwork and body positioning, then hours on the first two strike counters. You dropped your stick well that was 50 pushups, oh that guy did [strike] number two wrong, so everyone repeat number two 50 times!! You would go home and have to soak your hands, pop the blisters, your legs would be on fire, but that was the way or the path you took to be a "Stick Fighter." Remy had very little interest in teaching like that publicly.

When he stayed with my parents in the early 80s, I was fortunate enough because I had learned some Kali from my Wing Chun Do instructor and had some friends that learned what they called back then, Pekiti Tirsia Arnis. Whenever I saw something cool [that] they did, I would challenge Remy with it and he would show me counters and that began our training in traditional Eskrima. We, like the other traditional arts, would spend hours on body mechanics, weight shifting, getting the most power from short range, using a longer stick but yet getting closer to nullify your opponent's power. Learning that all the fancy traps and stuff were just to get you used to seeing things from all different angles, and of course, the block and lock [DA note: blocking and capturing the stick] that was the core of Remy's stick fighting.

Professor Dan Anderson, I don't know if you are aware of that, but you were part of that history, one of the earliest times he ever taught what he later coined Tapi Tapi was at your 1985 summer camp, if you remember we spent a whole day on countering the counters and then some of us were countering the counters to the counters.

Remy was and always will be one of the greatest innovators in the martial arts world. He constantly changed with the times, I believe had he lived he was going to come almost full circle. I believe he would have found a way to teach even more of his fundamentals that he learned in his youth. His students were opening up to more and more of the core stuff. Many were hungry. They wanted that fighting stuff that he had learned. They wanted to become Eskrimadors. Some did, but many more wanted to and some still are seeking out the many forms of Balintawak, for example. They see little things in that art that they have seen in the Modern Arnis training.

Yep, the "Old Man" left a treasure map of sorts. Some are taking that map and following the clues. It's all there. You just have to know how to find it and test it and make it yours, because after all, it's all "THE ART WITHIN YOUR ART."

Thank you, Rocky,
Super Dan

An Introduction To Modern Arnis – Fred King

(This second essay is an excerpt from an interview I did with Fred King, the martial artist who introduced me to Prof. Remy. This is a beautiful combination of warrior spirit and deep friendship.)

Leonard Trigg, My understanding is Leonard was the first who brought him into the NW and I was the first school he brought him to. I think 1978, 1979, someplace in there, Leonard brought him over one day. I was in the middle of my afternoon, he says, "Fred, I want to introduce you to, to Remy Presas." And he did.

The Professor explained to me what Arnis was about as I didn't know anything about it. He explained it was knife and stick fighting and you know I'm Kajukenbo and I was definitely familiar with knife and stick fighting. We started to talk and I found he was very friendly guy, very nice. Unpretentious. And then he said, "I show you the knife. I show you arnis. You have a knife" I said "Yeah, I have a knife.

So I grabbed a knife and then he says, "You stick me, you stick." So I, you know, [Fred makes the motion of stabbing forward hesitantly]. He said, "Oh no, no, take off the cover." So, I took the cover off. It was now a live blade. And he goes, "Yes, stick me with the knife." So, I kind of went [moves at a medium fast speed] as I would with a green belt. And it was live. It was pointed. It was sharp.

I stuck at him. He grabbed it and he goes, "No, no much faster, much faster." And I remember this, I was using my left. I do a flip to my right [hand] and he says "Yeah." and I stuck like this [He timed the stab when Remy started to speak and this time he did it quickly.] I'm holding it tight enough not to lose it but loose enough for speed and poke/slicing.

He did [something] which I've seen on TV, you know, the scissors. [DA note: This is where one hand strikes the back of the hand holding the knife while the other hits wrist.] I was moving at a good rate of speed and his hands were down to the sides.

The knife went across the room about 18 feet. I can feel my facial expression of "What?" I know my mouth, because I was like [demonstrates jaw being dropped], you know, I couldn't believe that just happened. I remember him doing it. I remember his smile and I remember me turning, watching the knife bounce on the floor. I went, I looked over Leonard and I said, "Okay, I'm in." That was my introduction to Professor Remy Presas.

He was a Master in Arnis, but more important to me, he was a good person and he loved what he did and the people he taught. He taught with a high level of competency and care for the student.

He originally introduced me to Professor Wally Jay as they were new friends. They would come to Portland together many times. I was to intimately watch the development of two masters in their own Art connect, exchange and help each other over the next 20 years. It taught me how love of The Art by Masters surpassed ego. They developed each other. I was to watch over those years as they explained and interchanged ideas with each other - with me only acting as their uke. Now that was enlightening, though quite painful (laughing).

The Professor and I were talking and I was always trying to pump him on reality fights. I said something about the reality of that and he goes, *"Freddy. Freddy. You have to keep it simple. You must keep it simple. You know how you like to fight in this distance and like to also, you know come in like this. That's what I do, I just do this* [showing a quick wrist flick in the motion of the "up

Prof. Remy & Fred King

and down" striking action]. *The person comes and I just do this, oh, because I catch them."* That was his big thing, keeping it simple. There was reality. And that was one of his big things. Simple and timing.

I wanted to feel the warrior spirit in him - and I was lucky and did. Whether we were drilling, free sparring or doing sparking swords (wow- those were eventful moments) it was there. And you could feel it. Even with that big smile. He was a warrior. And, as important, I felt the love that he had. When I trained alone with Prof. Presas and fought - and yes, he would fight - his attitude was not as benign, especially if I was overly aggressive - and I was. But he always ended it with a laugh and me better understanding my weaknesses. And with cuts and some abrasions. Not him. (lol)

(I asked Fred this question, *"How did the old man impact your art? How did he impact Fred King?"*)

On a martial basis I break it into three things.

One of them, and you touched on it - his certainty level was extremely high. And he would test himself with me, allowing me my strengths and he would do his weak links (whatever they were, I couldn't see them). He was humble and his certainty level was he would try things and do things untested. Even today I test myself with others people. I'll go work with jujitsu guys who can rip me a new asshole on the ground. Yeah, and you know, a boxer who can outbox me and all those kinds of stuff but you're testing your art within the context of your art, and against theirs. And it's cool. And he gave me that. Test - be humble. And be willing to get your ass kicked.

Professor had such certainty on what he did, there was no question about it. And that's why I think it's sort of like, the last great Aikido master, Ueshiba. He could do it he what he taught. I think what he taught is what he was doing but people didn't have the stepping stones.

The second thing, I think that was part of what the Professor wanted to do, was to give people more stepping stones, so they could come to where he was at. He could break things down well and into little pieces for people. He was doing more and more of that as time went on. When I was typically working with him he would break it down but it was always fast and rough.

The third thing I learned was to flow. When I first met him, he and Professor Jay would talk about the flow in a little different context. But when they merge together you can tell; you can see how they were interacting so beautifully there.

So, there was certainty, there was the flow and then there was... move from one thing to another. Constant motion of technique with your partner, never stopping, never forcing too much but flowing from one thing to the next. Both of them

Prof. Wally Jay

talked and showed me how they did it. I could see it and they were so much in love with their Art. It was a beautiful thing.

Beautiful revelation for me. The Flow. There's a circular action because it gives you an ability to be more certain, to be able to flow with one technique to the next, and then you know it's a "now" thing. It becomes spontaneous, practical and creative all at the same time. I've haven't been asked that question before, but those are the three things that the Professor gave to me here are really important.

We were really good friends. We would talk for hours about all types of things. Personal, family, training modern arnis - I was his confidant. You know, I was his friend. I mean a good friend of martial tradition. Yeah, he was my teacher but we'd talk about all kinds of stuff. We would just have *conversations*. We had a connection because this guy was a warrior. He had a big smile on his face. People think if you smile you show weakness... nahhhhhh, he was a warrior. And I love that. There are many who know Modern Arnis better than I, they can teach it better and have a better understanding of it that's for sure. What I knew was the man, and I loved the man, and I received back the same.

All right, back to my Facebook posts.

The Future of Modern Arnis part 1

Am I worried about the future of Modern Arnis? No, but not for the reason one might think. I am a student of history and what does history tell us? That civilizations and cultures are fragile things.

They do not endure. Look at the empire of Rome. Where is it today? Well, Rome is located in pretty much the same spot but the Roman empire is long gone. Does the British empire still exist? Nope. The UK is still in the same spot but in a very different condition. It is not a continent spanning empire that rules the seas.

Civilizations and cultures are fragile things. They do not endure.

Martial arts are a very small sub-culture of a planetary culture. They morph and change with each passing year. Modern Arnis is the same. The art Prof. Remy left us 20-ish years ago is not the art being taught today. It has morphed and changed in the last two decades and will continue to do so in the next two decades and more. Maybe the name will die out. Maybe it won't. Who knows?

Am I worried about the future of Modern Arnis? Not in the slightest. I am a student of history and history tells me that it will not, in the long run, endure. All of Prof. Remy's senior students and the upcoming generations will do what we can to honor the founder, each in our own unique ways. Mine is through books and videos.

Will Modern Arnis endure through the generations? No. What was the name of the art that Remy's grandfather, Leon, learned outside of a generic title such as baston, etc.? Things change. They morph. They die out. Thus is the way of history.
Super Dan

The Future of Modern Arnis part 2

This is a follow up to my brief essay of yesterday. There has a bit of yip about who is doing "pure" Modern Arnis vs "tainted" Modern Arnis lately and part 1 of this essay was an answer to that bit of nonsense. If civilizations and cultures (including martial arts sub-cultures) do not endure, then why bother?

Ahhhhhhhh, there are very good reasons to bother. Many of us have gotten the same gifts from various instructors. I will keep this to my teacher, Remy Presas. If Modern Arnis is going to change and morph over the years and end up barely resembling what RP taught, how do we keep it going? There are two aspects that I stress – preserving the spirit of the art and preserving the essence of the art.

Hanshi Bruce Juchnik told me over the phone this phrase – *"If you want to preserve the art, preserve the spirit."* Beautifully stated. So, what is the spirit of Modern Arnis? For me, it is the spirit of presenting a way for anyone to exceed their expectations. This is what Remy Presas did for me. The spirit of Modern Arnis may be different from one to the next and that is rightly so. He touched thousands of martial artists over the years.

What is the essence of Modern Arnis? The Flow. The Flow is in everything Modern Arnis. Modern Arnis is not the same without the Flow.

What about specific techniques? After 55 years active participation in the martial arts and four 10th Dan certificates (Karate: Allen Steen & J. Pat Burleson, Modern Arnis: Presas Arnis Legacy – Roberto Presas & International Modern Arnis of The Philippines) I can say this – techniques are a dime a dozen. I have found so many common threads, technique wise, in the various martial arts that there are no "special moves" or "secret applications." I remember Chuck Norris telling me when I was an under belt *"There are only so many ways to move the human body."* I would add that there are only a finite number of applications.

So, to me the future of Modern Arnis lies in preserving the spirit and essence of the art. What about "pure Modern Arnis?" To paraphrase Ed Parker, *"When pure stick meets pure head, you have pure Modern Arnis."*
Super Dan

The Future of Modern Arnis part 3

"If you want to preserve the art, preserve the spirit."
Hanshi Bruce Juchnik

Perfect words. Civilizations and cultures and subcultures do not endure but the spirit does. The spirit of Modern Arnis – what is it? I can only answer for me.

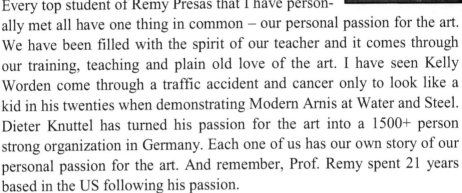

Bruce Juchnik

The personal passion for the art.
Every top student of Remy Presas that I have personally met all have one thing in common – our personal passion for the art. We have been filled with the spirit of our teacher and it comes through our training, teaching and plain old love of the art. I have seen Kelly Worden come through a traffic accident and cancer only to look like a kid in his twenties when demonstrating Modern Arnis at Water and Steel. Dieter Knuttel has turned his passion for the art into a 1500+ person strong organization in Germany. Each one of us has our own story of our personal passion for the art. And remember, Prof. Remy spent 21 years based in the US following his passion.

The enthusiasm for teaching the art.
If you watch Bruce Chiu or Roland Rivera or Bram Frank teaching, you will see a reflection of Prof. Remy's enthusiasm. Dieter Knuttel is living lightning on the floor. Brian Zawilinski is rather quiet until he takes the floor and then he becomes very animated. Those of us OG's, original gangsters, remember very well how enthusiastic Prof. Remy would get when he was teaching us.

The joy or aesthetic of movement.
Tim Gustavson once said to me *"There is a joy in movement."* Beautifully stated. Beyond the combat applications of Modern Arnis there is the joy and aesthetic of movement. Couple this with co-motion. What do I mean by that? Why do students love the sinawali drills, 6-count, give and take drills, the Tapi-Tapi configurations, the semi-free sparring patterns? In all of them there is the aspect of co-motion, moving in concert with another. This is something that we humans share, an affinity for co-motion. Add into this all of the solo drills and anyos (forms) and you have movement.

28

These are just the points of the spirit of Modern Arnis that I am aligned with. These are the points I strive to preserve. *"If you want to preserve the art, preserve the spirit."*
Super Dan

The Future of Modern Arnis part 4
In my last essay I talked about preserving the spirit of the art. This essay is about preserving the essence of Modern Arnis.

> *Essence* definition: [dictionary.com] noun 1. the basic, real, and invariable nature of a thing or its significant individual feature or features.

For me, the essence of Modern Arnis is the FLOW. A flow is an unending stream of smooth and fluid motion. A dictionary definition of flow is: *a steady continuous stream of something*. I was very familiar with the start-stop qualities of karate kata. I began my entry in the flow with combinations on the open point fighting circuit. That jumped to a whole new level when I began Modern Arnis.

At first it was the basic flow drill. Then Give and Take. Then 6-count. And another and another and another. Everything was flow based, nothing staccato. Constant movement with your partner. There was something special about it. It took me decades to figure it out but there is one key aspect of flow drills that is overlooked by most practitioners – that of "co-motion."

Co-motion is the harmonious interaction between two or more people. This is something natural and enjoyable. I always wondered why everybody loved the countless sinawali drills. Patterns upon endless patterns of clacking sticks. As you might imagine, I was never a big fan of them but so many are. It's co-motion. This is natural amongst people.

Back to the flow. Is it specific to Modern Arnis or Filipino martial arts? Absolutely not. Watch Michael Jordon or Larry Bird (I'm sure showing my age) on the court. The flow. Watch a champion ice skater on the rink. The flow. Watch a champion gymnast doing a floor exercise. The flow.

So, why is the flow the essence of Modern Arnis? Technically it is the connecting thread to every action of Modern Arnis. It is counter the counter, the Tapi-Tapi, semi-free sparring, everything boiled down to one descriptive word.

Why is the flow so special to me? At the time of this writing I am pushing 70 years old. I keep getting comments like "You're still moving well for your age." Why is that? The flow of Modern Arnis has kept my body young and supple. Where I see others nowhere near to my age hobbling around, overweight, or struggling with bad joints, I am bouncing around like a kid. Last year I did a cross-country Spyder ride (think three-wheeled motor-cycle) to teach at the Connecticut camp. How in the heck did I manage that? The Flow.

So, in everything I write or video, I work to preserve that precious gift that Prof. Remy gave to me and thousands of others – the Flow.

In closing, Modern Arnis as a technical curriculum may not endure the coming decades. The spirit and essence of it, however, will continue on for quite some time. As will the name. There is no "pure" Modern Arnis. That left us in August 2001 with the passing of Remy Presas. But there is pure spirit and essence. That will go on and on and on.
Super Dan

Who Is <u>THE</u> Grandmaster Of Modern Arnis?
This is an interesting and inflammatory topic to some and a complete non-issue to others but it is one I'll chime in on. One Modern Arnis practitioner flatly states that there is only one GM of Modern Arnis and that was Remy Presas. That's all nice and fine except for two reasons:

1. Remy retired after his brain tumor diagnosis in (I believe) 2000, and
2. He passed away in 2001 leaving the door open for future GMs.

So, who is the king of the hill, the Modern Arnis hill anyway? Let's address these points one by one.

1. Actually, after he retired he could have been considered "Grandmaster emeritus." Here is a description of what an emeritus is from Stavros McCrakis, PhD Harvard, posted a year ago in Quora Digest:

> "*Emeritus* is used in academia to mean 'retired'. Some institutions confer it on all retired full professors. Others reserve it as a special honor. In either case, it is a way of saying that the professor remains an esteemed member of the academic community, even if he/she is no longer active.
>
> "After a person's death, there is no need to say that a person is retired. Just as we don't say that Henry Ford (1863–1947) was the former president or the retired president of Ford, we don't say that Paul Samuelson (1915–2009) was a professor emeritus at MIT.
>
> "The only case where someone may be called a professor emeritus after death is in an obituary, where it is referring to their status at the time of death. Otherwise, they should just be called professor after their death."

Now, whether one wants to accept that in a martial arts sense is up to them. But, Remy Presas did retire, leaving the Masters of Tapi-Tapi fill in for him at IMAF events.

2. With the passing of RP in 2001, that left an opening for others to be awarded that title. There is nothing official out there stated by Prof. Remy himself that the title is retained by only him after his passing or that others cannot attain it. Some may vehemently protest this but that protest and $5.00 will get you a cup of coffee.

So, who is THE grandmaster of Modern Arnis? No one. The article "the" indicates numerically one. There is no ONE. There are a number of Modern Arnis GMs depending on which organization is calling the shots.

In my opinion, all good. Each person who has contributed to the growth in their own way and capacity should be acknowledged and not be held to one person's arbitrary standard.

I think if Remy were here today and looked past any of the squabbles that still exist in the art, he'd be happy that the art remains extant and that there are a number of organizations, groups and individuals carrying it forward.

Super Dan

Prequel – Grandmaster…Where Did That Come From, Anyway?

You know how a movie like Star Wars turns into a blockbuster and then Hollywood makes moves that set up that one? They call them "prequels" as opposed to sequels (follow ups). This essay is a fresh one and a prequel to the one you just read.

Grand Master or Grandmaster? Where in the heck did that one come from? Back in the ancient days when I was a white belt, no one even dared to call themselves a master let alone a grand master. Sensei, sifu, sa bum nim were all accepted titles. In Japan there were terms initiated by the Budokan organization:

- Renshi ("polished teacher," 5th dan),
- Shihan ("quality instructor," 5th dan),
- Kyoshi ("expert teacher" 6th or 7th dan), and
- Hanshi ("exemplary teacher," 8th dan).

We in the States were gringos and never got these in the early days.

Then, out of the blue, the term "Grand Master" appeared. I have searched all over to find out who first used the term but much like ivy, once it caught hold it began to flourish. The term itself has an interesting etymology (definition: *the study of the origin of words and the way in which their meanings have changed throughout history*). This is from etymonline.com:

> grandmaster (n.)
> as a chess title, 1927, from grand (adj.) in the sense "chief, principal" + master (n.). Earlier (as two words) a title in Freemasonry (1724) and in military orders of knighthood (1550s).

The Merriam-Webster Dictionary defines *grandmaster* as:
> 1: the chief officer of a principal lodge in various fraternal orders (such as Freemasonry)
> 2: an expert player (as of chess) who has consistently scored high in international competition

The chess definition reminds me of a funny moment in the mockumentary *A Mighty Wind* where Jonathon Steinbloom (played by Bob Balaban) said to the interviewer, *"And I was a member of the chess team and whenever we would have chess tournaments I had to wear a protective helmet, I had to wear a football helmet."* I cracked up on that one – full contact chess! Okay, back on track.

Like I said, I have no clue who first took on the title of grandmaster in martial arts but it has blossomed into senior grand master, great grand master, founding grand master. Oy! What is coming next? The highest title keeps getting higher and higher it appears.

On a more serious note (and this subject gets very serious at times), Punong Guro Edgar Sulite (September 25, 1957 – April 10, 1997) wrote this in his book *Masters of Arnis, Kali and Eskrima.*

What Makes A Grandmaster? By Punong Guro Edgar G. Sulite
Thursday, September 29th, 1994

To be recognized as a Grandmaster or Master of combat arts in the Philippines, you must have made your reputation and show mental maturity and physical age. Grandmasters question the rankings of other grandmasters.

Masters and grandmasters are criticized and questioned regarding their skills and abilities. Who bestowed their title? Do they have enough skills for the titles they carry? How many years have they been practicing the art? How old is he? How many followers and students does this man have?

In other martial arts, the attainment of a certain level automatically designates the title Master or Grandmaster. In the Philippines, there are certain norms to be satisfied before one can be called and accepted as a Master or Grandmaster.

A master of the art must be a master of himself. He must be in control. His daily life epitomizes a man in control of his life, his destiny. A master of the art must know his art, its origins, its history, its philosophy. He must know the techniques, the interplay of techniques, and the reversals of techniques.

A master must know the basics, the intermediate forms and techniques, and the advanced levels of the art. Mastery of the art does not only mean so many years in the art, but the amount of experience using the art, one's personal evolution within the art and personal dedication and contribution to the art.

Punong Guro Edgar Sulite

A master of the art must know how to teach and impart knowledge from the art. He must be able to communicate, elaborate and present the art in such a way that each student learns on a personal basis. Each instruction is adapted to the learning process and ability of the student. A master must be a real maestro, a real teacher.

A master of the art must be of good character. He should epitomize the qualities of a leader, the majesty of a noble, and the courage and strength of a warrior.

A master of the art is called and acknowledged a Master by other masters, never by himself.

Punong Guro Edgar G. Sulite
Lameco Eskrima

I like it. The fascinating thing is that nowhere in this essay of his does he say there is only one grand master per art or lineage. I think this whole "who's on first" business comes out of small-mindedness and ego. Is this the pot calling the kettle black? It might be. Been there, done that, outgrew that.

So, back to the preceding essay on Who Is THE Grand Master of Modern Arnis? No one. Who are the Grand Masters of Modern Arnis? Let's see. Off the top of my head:

Rene Tongson
(IMAFP & Presas Legacy)
Rodel Dagooc
(IMAFP & Presas Legacy)
Jeremiah DeLa Cruz
(IMAFP & Presas Legacy)
Samuel "Bambit" Dulay
(IMAFP & Presas Legacy)
Dieter Knuttel
(IMAFP & Presas Legacy)

Dan Anderson
(IMAFP & Presas Legacy)
Kelly Worden
(IMAFP & Presas Legacy)
Brian Zawilinski
(IMAFP & Presas Legacy)
Brian Johns (IMAF)
Earl Tullis (IMAF)
Astrid Zimdahl (IMAF)

And those are just the ones off the top of my head. There may be more. It's hard to keep track. My thoughts on the matter? Ahhhhhhh, it's time to get back to training.

Titles In Modern Arnis...And What Do They Mean?
(I found this essay recently. I wrote it roughly five years before the preceding essays. It fits in well here.)

One interesting point of distinction has been the awarding of titles by Prof. Remy. There have been all sorts of interpretations of what each title means and how it rates in the hierarchy and there is one thing everybody agrees on – whatever title they have, they like it.

It began, I believe, with the Datu title. What was a Datu? What did it mean? Well, "Datu" translates to "chieftain, chief of the tribe" and so forth. Shishir Inocalla, originally a student of Pepito Robas, was the first Datu in Modern Arnis. He was followed by Kelly Worden, Ric Jornales, Dieter Knuttel, David Hoffman and Tim Hartman.

Since the passing of Prof. Presas, a couple of the Datus are no longer active in Modern Arnis. Ric Jornales teaches the Jornales Sikaran system and David Hoffman has since died. The remaining Datus have not passed that title on to any other practitioners of Modern Arnis.

In the last 10 or so years the Remy Presas Black Bell Hall of Fame Foundation has awarded the Datu title to Tom Bolden, Doug Pierre and Bram Frank. This has caused a bit of controversy among the initial Datus. It got so hot that I finally posted up on Facebook my thoughts on the subject. (Note: I received the Datu title from the Foundation in 2020.)

June 24, 2016 – I hate to be the voice of sobriety here but seeing the amount of steam that has arisen from three different threads (Michelle Ralston's congratulations to Bram Frank, Shishir Inocalla's posts, and Tim Hartman's video post), I figured to post one more time on the subject.

1. Unity of Modern Arnis is going to be like unity of Shotokan karate or Aikido or Systema or Wing Chun or Goju-ryu or Ed Parker Kenpo

Karate. Every branch of Shotokan whether it is Shigeru Egami's Shotokai, Hirokazu Kanazawa's Shotokan International, Hidetaka Nishiyama's All-America Karate Federation they all acknowledge Funakoshi Gichin as the founder.

These are just the most prominent examples. You have the same with Aikido, Systema, Goju-ryu karate, Wing Chun or EPAK or, or, or... The founder is known and recognized and the following generations go on their way. This is historical fact and the nature of people.

Go to Wikipedia and you'll find for Goju-Ryu 19 different organizations. Shotokan shows 6 descendent schools. Aikido has Yoshinkan (Gozo Shioda), Yoseikan (Minoru Mochizuki), Shodokan (Kenji Tomiki), Iwami Ryu (Morihiro Saito), and Ki Society (Koichi Tohei).

And so on.

2. Does anybody know how many branches of Modern Arnis there are out there? Doing the research for my most recent book set (*The Complete Dan Anderson Encyclopedia of Modern Arnis*) I have found 19 different groups AND I bet I am missing more. There hasn't been "one Modern Arnis" since Prof. Remy's death in 2001.

3. Each branch of the above martial arts uses their own titles. How many Shihans are there out there? Renshis? Hanshis? How many grandmasters? Lots. Who gave who the title is no longer the question but do they deserve it is the key. And who decides that? The hierarchy in the individual organizations do. That's who.

Historically speaking each art begins as one art under the founder and when the founder dies (and sometimes before), branches occur. Again, human nature. And you believe that there has not been contention, go back over the history of American Kenpo or the split between the Honbu Dojo of Aikido and Koichi Toihei for starters.

4. Remy has been not been with us for 15 years.

Whether he would approve someone being titled a Datu at this point in time is really a moot point. I'm sorry to be so blunt about it but it is fact. Remy is not here to approve or disapprove anything. The question of "What would Remy do?" has actually been a moot point for the same period of time.

As to whether one needs permission from the datus to issue a datu recognition - that is not going to happen for two reasons. Why? Because 3 of the 6 datus have already stated that only Remy could appoint it and because none of the 19 branches of Modern Arnis that I have found have the same leader. Honestly, who is going to agree on who can do what, especially in the area of restrictions? Not many.

I know the passion for the art many of the conflicting players have. The passion is real. The journeys are different and the future paths will be different.

The Remy Presas Black Belt Hall of Fame Foundation awarding of the title of datu is here to stay. The objection to this by the Remy Presas datus is probably also here to stay. Let's move on.
Super Dan

What Is Modern Arnis?
(This is the transcript of the lecture I gave at the Remy Presas Legacy Camp, Connecticut 2021. It was the second day of the camp and my turn to teach. I have been to many, many camps and quite often a brief respite is needed and wanted for the attendees to remain fresh for the rest of the camp. So, instead of physically training, I delivered the following lecture. It is pretty much word for word and edited only in a few spots to make for easier reading.)

Okay, so you guys having a good time? Yeah, I haven't. I haven't been as excited about a camp like this since 2005. And, you know, Roland was there and Jimmy was there. And it was it was a camp that I and a student of Bob Quinn's, Dee Childress put on. And we had a number of masters in there. And it was just rock and roll from the very, from the get go.

And there's something special that I wanted to do today. And I wanted to break up the training, because it's very, very easy to get into information overload. And so instead of, you know, okay, now we're going to do this move that move in the next move. It's kind of okay, let's chill out. Let's relax. Let's get our minds going in a different direction. And the direction that I want to go over is *"What is Modern Arnis?"* And I think this is especially a good point [in time], since this is the 20th anniversary of Professor Remy's death.

First thing is, okay, who am I to do deliver a dissertation on *"What Is Modern Arnis?"* So I'm just going to give you just very, very brief credentials. When I met Professor Remy, I was already a four time national karate champion. My nickname was *Super Dan*. I was known, I found out later, throughout the world, not throughout the country, I found out later in the 80s that people knew me as Super Dan in not only Canada, but Europe and so forth, which, you know, is quite gratifying. But I had 14 years of world class skills under my belt.

And then I met Professor Remy. Janet [Aalfs] and I were talking about timing. Sometimes when the right thing comes into your life, it's also it's perfectly timed. I was heading into the end of my competitive career. And it was like, *"Okay, what next?"* I was a karate jock. I was a voracious studier of martial arts history but practitioner wise, I was a karate jock. And then I met Professor Remy and, as I've said to many, many people in the past, he opened up the world, because there was a lot to martial arts that I did not know about. He was the key person for my transformation from being a karate jock to a martial artist.

So for the 21 years, since I met him, he was my sole teacher in Modern Arnis. And I was a *seminar rat*, and I use that term lovingly. I went to seminar, seminar, seminar, because he didn't have a home dojo. He didn't have a centralized dojo. He did not have a linear curriculum. What we had was we had the technical list that was at the camps and everybody did the same thing. You either moved up to the next belt rank, or if the Professor was putting you up for black, than you were black, but you did the same thing that everybody else did. You just either did it better, faster, stronger, or whatever.

So now this year, this summer marks the 20th anniversary of Professor Remy's death. And that's the keynote thrust of this camp. I see people from different eras. I see a lot of you guys. I'm pleased. I'm really pleased to see you guys here. There are several people who are old timers that I had never met. I finally got to meet Bruce Chiu. I finally got to meet Larry Rocha. You know, guys who are household names in Modern Arnis but our paths always, like two ships passing, didn't happen.

So I look at arnis, I look at it in a comparative(way). One can look at arnis, let's say, as how it relates to another art, painting. Well, maybe to them, arnis is like Rockwell. Maybe it's like Jackson Pollock. How does it jibe to the person? With me, it's music. To me, this (arnis) is jazz. Now, when you listen to jazz and you look at the entire spectrum of jazz, what you have is you have rhythm, you have flow, you have innovation, you have improvisation. You have steady beat, you have syncopated beats. You have all of this, that goes here and there, (I) kind of start to get animated. I just love it.

But to me, it's jazz. And especially when you start getting into the free flow, man, that's where you start. If you look at all the different drills that we have done, to me, they are tunes you've learned, chord progressions, they are your scales, so that you can sit down, and whether you're a guitar, trumpet, piano player, you can play. And then when you get good. You and I you play a duet. Now you're playing off of somebody else. And this is just utterly fascinating to me now.

How many here have not have not listened to Miles Davis? Anybody did not listen to Miles Davis? (Somebody raises their hand.) Okay. Thank you. You have not lived a full life. (laughter) You have not lived a complete life, in my estimation. Miles Davis. He changed the face of jazz no less than five times during his lifetime. Now, if you think about any pop singer, or country singer, whatever, who changes that direction of the genre during their lifetime? Let's take Garth Brooks. Okay, country.

Incredible, incredible performer. From everything I see, wonderful human being. He has not changed the face of country five times. The Beatles? Maybe twice. First when they were the little mop tops and doing pop music that was based on American R&B. And then when they got into their psychedelic era, and they started spacing. Okay. That's two times.

Miles Davis, five times. Remy Presas, to me, is the Miles Davis of Modern Arnis.

When I talk about (this), I'm going to go back and forth between jazz and arnis to really tie them together. But when we talk about, let's say, Miles, changing the face of jazz in the 1940s, what was prevalent was bebop. Bebop is fast, it is has complex harmonies, complex rhythm, speed. Art Tatum. Dizzy Gillespie. Charlie Parker. Wow, just ripping and tearing. In 1950 Miles puts together this, either seven piece or nine piece (band). I can't remember. But he starts putting out smooth, relaxed jazz.

Relaxed - what people think is like West Coast jazz and it's just it calms stuff down. And people start shifting towards that. I think the most notable proponent is a fellow named Chet Baker, who played this smooth jazz. Well, Miles was before him. Miles.

Check it out. There's an album called *The Birth of the Cool* and it took jazz off in this direction.

Then he shifts from that to what is called hard bop. Now hard bop is different than bebop in that it incorporates gospel rhythms, rhythm & blues influences, blues, and a tiny bit of free-form improv, not much, but we're off of this smooth thing back into this little harder edge thing. Now you're starting to hear certain things that you're familiar with if you listen to other music. This is with his first great quintet who most notably had with him on tenor and soprano sax; John Coltrane (photo below left). And most jazz people sit back, *"Trane - you better believe it? Yeah."*

But it's the next shift. That really I want to tie in with what Remy Presas did and that is in 1968. He started introducing electric instruments into his jazz model. And it started off with (an album called) *In a Silent Way*. It moved there drastically to *Bitches Brew*. Then it turns harder rock into *A Tribute to Jack Johnson*. And then (he) starts incorporating funk in *On The Corner*. He's four albums. Now, the fascinating thing is that on the album cover, and this is really significant in the comparison, on the album cover of *In a Silent Way*. It has a line in there: *Directions In Music by Miles Davis*.

Now, one thing Miles didn't like, he hated people calling his music jazz because it pigeonholed it. He didn't pigeonhole his music as jazz. Everybody else would call it jazz and genre wise, it fit into jazz. But Miles was being conceptual. He didn't think in terms of jazz. He thought in terms of music, and the influences that were coming in at the time. Okay, it's 1968, things start becoming more electrified, he starts pulling in the electric piano, he starts pulling in electric guitar and so forth. And while *In a Silent Way* was a very subtle shift, *Bitch's Brew* was a dead punch to the face. *Directions In Music*.

Let's shift back over to Remy Presas. Now, it's pretty well known that he got his start in Filipino Martial Arts is World War Two. His family moves up into the mountains. And dad (Jose Presas) is teaching the Filipino guerrillas, jungle fighters. And young Remy, when he's watching – he's five or six - he's fascinated. He goes and he pulls a switch off the tree and he starts imitating the movements. The side by side and the figure eight, and he's whacking all the leaves. He's beating all the leaves off the tree and that sort of thing. His grandfather catches him; probably wasn't hard to catch him in, everything within reach is knocked down to the ground, says *"Remy, do you want to learn arnis?" "Yes." "Okay. I will teach you."* So Remy starts learning from his grandfather.

I won't go as far as saying that he learned the Presas family art because I cannot find anything in writing that says something is the Presas family art. But my thinky-think, and I'll label *opinion* at any point in time when I think it's opinion and I can't back it up (in documentation). But my thinky-think is grandpa taught dad (Jose) and dad taught others and Remy spied on Dad and that's how he started learning. But he did learn from his granddad. Okay, I have all this cataloged in the book that I brought. And I want a special tip of the hat to Joe Rebelo. His interview with Remy Presas, the last videoed interview with Remy Presas, was one of the sources of Remy's history in his own words. So I'm not taking somebody else's writing, somebody else's article, we're talking. I got the interview. I had it transcribed. And then with headphones on, I corrected the transcription along with another interview. I did it anyway, to come out with a linear timeline of Professor Remy's upbringing, his training and so forth.

So we all know that he trained with his grandfather. This is verified by many other sources. He moves to Cebu or goes over to Cebu. He's 14 years old and goes over with, I think, a cousin or friend of his. And then he hooks up with the next source of Filipino martial art which is balintawak eskrima. And what is interesting in his accounting of meeting with Rodolfo Mongcol is him saying *"They cannot catch me. I am moving. I am slashing. I will not stand. I do not stand still."* Okay, what is he doing? He's doing, as Uncle Bram (Frank) would say, a cutting art. He's moving. He's angling. Balintawak is bit more of a forward-backward stick dueling system. They like him because he's got guts.

From 1950 to 1957. He trains in balintawak eskrima. First learns under Rodolfo Mongcol. Then he graduates to Timoteo Maranga. Finally graduates to the founder of balintawak, Anciong Bacon. And while he's doing this, you know, obviously he's gaining the skills but the fascinating thing is the bedrock of what he has is also the blade art. Interesting marriage. Interesting marriage. Now, in 1957, he decides for one lifesaving reason and probably for other reasons, he's leaving Cebu.

And a fascinating thing is in 1957 - remember, I talked about Miles Davis, Directions In Music - in 1957, he (Remy) has a vision of where he wants to go with this already. He knows where he wants to go. He tells his teacher *"When I start teaching, I am not going to teach your system. I am not going to teach stick fighting. I'm going to teach for physical education and self-defense."* They part on good terms. Remy leaves.

Directions In Music by Miles Davis. *Directions in Arnis by Remy Presas.*

Okay, they're running a parallel path. So if he's going into new directions, what was the old direction? Oh, that was interesting, interesting research. I have an essay by Krishna Godhania in *Modern Arnis – The Martial Art of Remy Presas*). Krishna is not a Modern Arnis person and he's talking about Filipino duels and arnis. To be very kind about it, it had a bad rep. Arnis, eskrima had bad PR. Dockworkers, ruffians, bodyguards - basically roughnecks and thugs. That's who did arnis. That's the PR. What was the huge martial arts interest in the Philippines? Karate, Judo, Taekwondo. How come? They were clean. Everybody dressed the same. They had the white jammies. They had the belts. They had the curriculum. They all did the same thing at the same time. Whoohoo! Things were organized. This was much more palatable than guys with sticks and knives who are going to put a noggin conk on you if they didn't like you.

Now, also, what was it used for? Okay, it was used for either dueling or fighting I mean, and when I say dueling or fighting I mean dueling or fighting. Anciong Bacon, founder of balintawak went to prison for killing somebody deader than a doornail. Antonio Ilustrisimo, "Tatang," he had several certified kills under his belt. There is a book by Dave Gould on Lameco eskrima talking about the founder, Jose Caballero. And this is a misquote, I've got the real quote into the book. He's talking about when you're practicing, if you're not practicing each strike hard enough to break somebody's skull, then why do it? That was arnis at the time.

Now, 1957, Remy is going to take a left turn at Albuquerque. He loves the art. He's going to figure out a way to clean up the art. So what does he do? He goes back to his hometown He actually starts a school. Then he goes back into Manila at the urging of, I believe, a mayor if I remember, right, (the nice thing is I've got it all written down so I don't have to remember a dadgum thing) but he gets into the school system. Now the fascinating thing is, in order to get into the school system, he first had to teach judo. And he had to sneak arnis in under the rug. But by this time, he has a curriculum. The book that you're about to receive (Prof. Remy's first book), many, many people do not know this but those are the requirements for first grade black in Modern Arnis. I've had this verified by three independent sources, one in the Philippines, two in the United States. He actually has a curriculum. He has organization.

One of the things that Mark Wiley had so artfully noted in an interview with Dean Franco on FMADiscussion was that he had exact blocks for exact strikes, exact disarms for exact strikes and so on. He actually had set up a curriculum. This hadn't been done before. And he was pushing more towards self-defense as opposed to stick fighting.

Now, when I when I look at self-defense and I look at fighting, those are two different animals. With me, self-defense is protection with fighting, "So let's get down! Let's, let's party because it's this is going to turn out really unfortunate for somebody." Well, Remy had enough of that. And trust me, he had been in a number of rumbles. I've got several that are actually outlined in the book (*Modern Arnis – The Martial Art of Remy Presas*). And he was he was a little bit of a roughneck and thug as well. There was a quote I just read recently and dadgum it, if I had found it, before publishing the book, I would have put it in the book, where he had stated that he was starting to get a reputation that if you want to train with him, you had to fight. And he wanted to change that rep.

So he's taking this art, which the underlying bedrock is survival and he wants to shift it.

Directions In Arnis just like *Directions In Music*.

Now, he comes to the United States. Okay. That is cataloged history. If you want to if you want to briefly state the history of Remy Presas in the United States, it was he went here and did a seminar. He went here and did a camp and he went here and did a seminar. And he took a break for two weeks. And he went here and did a seminar. And you do that for 21 years. And you have basically got the history of Remy Presas. Now, this is not talking about the developments because Modern Arnis developed as he was in the States and went through various stages. And I have those outlined as well so I'm not going to go through those.

But the thing that I look at when I when I make the comparison between Miles Davis and Remy Presas, I'm going to go back to Miles, you had this period of time where Miles was creating jazz rock. The critics had to come up with the term just to describe it because it was new music. At a certain point, a number of his key sidemen left him and formed their own bands.

One of the very first right off the bat, Tony Williams puts together *Tony Williams Lifetime.* He's got himself. He's got Larry Young on organ. He's got John McLaughlin on guitar and they were loud. They were energetic and they were poorly recorded but they were savage.

Herbie Hancock. He comes up with a septet, first a more freeform African/jazz music (*Mwandishi*) and then he slides over into funk-jazz, *Headhunters.*

Joe Zawinul and Wayne Shorter. Joe Zawinul was the only person who actually wrote tunes that were included on Bitches Brew. He was a keyboard player from Poland. Wayne Shorter was in the second great quintet of Miles. They teamed together to form their own music - *Weather Report*. Joe Zawinul is quoted *"Yeah, so what category are we in? We're Weather Report. That's the music we play."*

Chick Corea forms *Return To Forever*, a much slicker form than, let's say, the Mahavishnu Orchestra where I'll get to next. But he's got his own thing.

John McLaughlin, speed guitar par excellence, forms the *Mahavishnu Orchestra*.

Okay, then you get Billy Cobham, who did not come up with any particular name for his band other than him, Billy Cobham.

And who are these guys? They often refer to themselves as the *Children of Miles*. They came out of the Miles Davis lineage. And we have these very original types of jazz rock under their heading, but they came from Miles. And they never called themselves jazz.

It's 20 years since Remy passed. So who are the *Children of Remy*?

- Okay, I'll start with me. I'm a "child of Remy." I was his direct student for 21 years. I have an agreed upon by Remy, a subset of Modern Arnis that I just call the *MA80 System Arnis/Eskrima*. See that? Brian's got actually my shirt. I've got Brian's shirt on, he's got my shirt on. Okay, good. There's Tony Williams Lifetime.
- Then you've got Brian Zawilinski - *The Art Within Your Art*. Oh, you got Herbie Hancock over here.
- Then you have *Arnis International*. We have Bruce Chiu. Oh, we've got the Mahavishnu Orchestra over here.
- You got Roland Rivera – *Master of Tapi-Tapi*. Well, you got Billy Cobham over here.
- Bram Frank and *CSSD/SC Modular Knife*. Sounds like some Stanley Clarke action to me.

| Me & Brian | Bruce Chiu (L) | Roland Rivera | Bram Frank |

You have the *Children of Remy*; and what are all doing? We're all doing our own versions of Modern Arnis whether we strictly state that *"Yes, this is Modern Arnis or this is The Art Within Your Art. This is Arnis International or this is the MA80 System Arnis/Eskrima or, or, or..."* This is where the art continues. One of the earliest students in the United States, Bruce Juchnik and I could just kill him for this, only because he thought of it and I didn't. He said, *"If you want to preserve the art, preserve the spirit."* And those of us who train with Professor Remy, those of us who've been taught by Remy Presas know exactly what we're talking about as far as preserving the spirit.

So this is my question, what is Modern Arnis now? (I pick out several students in the group and ask them…)
"Hi, what's your name, dear?" (answers)
"Brianna, How old are you?" (answers)
"How long have you been doing Modern Arnis?" (answers)
"You are Modern Arnis." I ask a different person.

"How long have you been doing Modern Arnis?" (person answers)
"Say again, seven years?"
"Yeah, you are Modern Arnis and you're Modern Arnis and you're Modern Arnis (pointing to each person I say this to). *And you all are Modern Arnis. This is where the art is heading."*

There have been a couple of terms that have been introduced into the lexicon. That and we're going to go into personal opinion. They've been introduced. One has been the concept of a "first generation student." And there have been different definitions of first generation student or how you can work up to being a first generation student. Bobby Taboada (R) just recently had answered a statement by  Ising Attilo on YouTube. And he made a very, very poignant point. *"When I trained with the old masters, there was no talk of 'first generation'."* I'm sitting back and I'm going, *"You know, I never had I never heard Professor Remy ever say anything about first generation."* The closest thing he might have said about first generation would be, and I'm gonna take Dieter Knuttel as an example. He's a great friend of mine. He's in Germany, he (Remy) would say something like, *"Oh, Dieter, he studied to my brother Ernesto. But now he study with me."* And that's all he would say. Oh, he started with Ernesto. But now he's mine. Remy, if nothing else was inclusive.

I was talking with Tye (Botting). He originally studied with Eric Alexander. Now, I know Eric Alexander because I fought him twice in karate tournaments (photo right). And he came after me like I owed him money. He wanted some skin. And it was mine. (laughter) And I went against him twice. But they were wars. Tye started with Eric. So, was he a first generation student? Professor Remy's? Well, I asked him *"So who's your instructor?" "Professor Remy."* Yeah, that's right. That's right. Doesn't matter where you started because the old man accepted you. Didn't matter where you started. Didn't matter whether you started in some other eskrima or like me - I was just the karate jock. Like I said, he accepted you, you were his.

So I don't buy into the first generation talk. It's too easy to prop oneself up while pushing another down by using that. And Remy never said it.

Now, another term that's been introduced in the lexicon has been the term *"derivative."* Now, any of you guys who might know me is that I am just wicked mad on exact definitions. I'll give you the exact definition of Modern Arnis that Remy Presas did because I told you very, very early that there's only one time that I ever saw where gave a definition for Modern Arnis, however, but I'll do that in a moment.

   Derivative: noun, it is quote, *something that is based on another source.*

Well, in the words, my buddy, Bruce Chiu, bang! We're all based on another source. We're all derivative. Whether we are Modern Arnis or we're TAWA or whatever, we're based on Remy. Remy was taught by granddad and he was taught by his three Balintawak instructors, and any other influence including Cacoy Canete because he loved Cacoy's twirling, so he ripped off that twirling. That's in Joe Rebelo's interview. And he ripped off anybody that he could find because he was a sponge.

And I'll tell you right now, if you knew Prof. Remy before he met Prof. Wally Jay and then after he met Professor Wally Jay, all of a sudden the joint locks got really nasty a lot faster. Yeah, but he was a sponge that way.

So, we are all derivative. But the fascinating thing is did he ever use that term? No.

The only cataloged way he defined Modern Arnis is how he described it in Karate International Magazine, May/June issue 1989. The question was:

KIM - *"What is the difference between Modern Arnis and regular Arnis?"*

RP – *"Well, it is like in America, because you had mathematics today you have modern mathematics. Modern Arnis is more practical, easier and flexible. That is why it is called Modern Arnis. There is a system. There are rules to follow like today of modern English and modern mathematics. It is a simplified system that teachers know how to use both the stick or the same techniques empty handed. It is a very effective martial arts system."* End quote.

To me, that's Modern Arnis. As a personal opinion, I accept nobody else's definition because nobody else is the founder. Now, Bruce is going to give me a definition of Arnis International. I will accept that 100% because that's Arnis International. If I give you a definition of the MA80 System Arnis/Eskrima; okay. That's my definition. That's not Remy's definition of *his* art. That now is *my* art, an offshoot or off-branch or a "continuation of".

If we take a look at what he did - there was this art that was not well thought of in the Philippines. He went back and took a left turn at Albuquerque. Why? He loved the art. He did not love what he saw was occurring with the art, which was taekwondo, karate, and Judo outplaying his wonderful martial art. Okay. More people were doing those. There was this indigenous art that he loved (arnis). It had a bad rep. He wanted it to continue. And here's an interesting thing. Many of us old timers know this. At the end of your very first seminar, what did he tell us to do? *"Now you teach."* Oh, now you go to your school you teach? Yeah, he

51

wasn't worried about curriculum form or is this the correct angle, blah, blah, blah. He was worried about the continuation of the art, the propagation of the art. It's almost like *"You go teach. I'll smooth you guys out later."* Now, of course, we geeky Americans who grew up on the elementary school 12th grade system, good. We start doing the curriculum in a consecutive base or a cumulative basis, that sort of thing; in a graduated basis. Okay. He wasn't concerned with that. That was Modern Arnis. Now, we all have the curriculums in place. I've got mine. Bruce's got his. Roland's got his and so forth.

So, all of this is in place now. It's like what Hanshi Bruce said. *"If you want to preserve the art, preserve the spirit."*

This camp lives up to that concept *preserve the spirit*. I think better than anybody. You watch you watch us move. You watch Janet rolling, myself, Bram, Bruce; you watch us move. You'll see a connecting thread. We won't all necessarily move the same, but we don't move *that* differently. Okay. And the attitudes of each of the instructors. Without us sitting down and talking about it, it has been preserve the spirit. So we're the old buzzards - if you guys want to preserve the art, preserve the spirit, you guys. Because you're Modern Arnis.

I think you told me you're a beginner (addressing one of the camp attendees). Am I right? Yeah, well, you are Modern Arnis. How long have you trained? Couple months? Well, you're as much Modern Arnis as I am. I've been at it for 41 years. 56 years if you count overall martial arts, I think older than some of you have been alive.

The question – *"What is Modern Arnis?"* This is my opinion. This is coming from for better or for worse, the "village elder." Brian calls me *Unka Dan.* You hear Rene Tongson from the Philippines call me *Uncle Dan-Manong Dan.* It's a position. It doesn't necessarily elevate me. It's just…it's nice. It's like, yeah, one of the old buzzards and I'm the oldest buzzard here today in terms of Modern Arnis. But this is coming from an Uncle Dan perspective. Thank you very much for your very, very patient attention. End of lecture.

Remy Sayings/Aphorisms

An aphorism, by definition, is: *a concise observation that contains a general truth, such as, "if it ain't broke, don't fix it."* Prof. Remy had a number of things he would repeat during instruction, whether privately or in a seminar setting. Some of his sayings were directly to the point and some of them were maddening because they didn't make sense in the context of what we were practicing. They all ended up making sense when you came at it from *his* point of view but you had to get there first. These are, by no means, all of his sayings but they are the ones I remember best.

"It is all the same."

This is the first of the maddening aphorisms. Prof. Remy would be demonstrating a technique for the group and then he would go off into variation upon variation. He would do one after another and another and then end up with saying *"It is all the same."* What? You just demonstrated 10 variations of a particular move and now you're saying they're all the same? What gives? What does "it is all the same" actually mean, from a Dan perspective, anyway?

First off, every technique in Modern Arnis can be found elsewhere. A wrist lock is a wrist lock, a throw is a throw. Modern Arnis doesn't have a monopoly or patent on any particular technique. But there's more. Any one set up can lead off into a myriad of directions. Flowing locks, for example, typify this aphorism. You start your partner with one joint lock and his reaction sets him for the next action and so on. It all started from one position but ends up in another. *"It is all the same."*

"No matter where you are, you are there already."
This one drove me nuts as well until one morning after a seminar. We were in Frank Shekosky's living room and Prof. Remy was drilling with me the 6-Count Drill. This is one of the beginning flow drills in Modern Arnis consisting of a forehand strike (#1 or #3), downward strike (#12) and backhand strike (#4 or #8) done back and forth. He demonstrated what to do if your partner introduced a thrust to the belly (#5) into the mix. The light bulb went off over my head. Instead of being thrown off, it occurred to me what he was showing me. It was that no matter what position you were in, you always had an option – *"...you are there already."*

"If he touches you he is cut already."
What the hell do you mean by that? Here we are doing stick work and then he says that! How are you cut by a stick, for crying out loud? Much later in my training I researched his personal history. His grandfather, Leon, raised Remy in the art of the blade. This was during World War ll. His father, Jose, was teaching Filipino guerillas to fight in the jungle. Young Remy was being taught how to survive, not sport or simple self-defense. This was the reality of the time. Obviously, those early lessons stuck with him throughout his life. Much later on, despite him teaching predominantly stick work in seminars, he was still thinking blade. Understanding the context of his early training, this now made sense.

"If your right hand can do it, so can your left."
Okay, this one was very easy to understand but a bit maddening in practice. Most of us are right handed. Prof. Remy was left handed. He was very, very good with his right hand stick applications but put the stick in his left hand, he was even better. I don't know about everybody else but
working the stick in my left hand took some doing. Putting a weapon in your non-dominant hand and utilizing it skillfully – that takes dedicated training! It took a while but I got the hang of it.

"But in real…"

Prof. Remy has been criticized by some for teaching only self-defense or the art side of Modern Arnis, especially since the advent of competitive arnis and eskrima competitions. To be fair, he was interested in spreading Filipino culture and not stick fighting/dueling. I use the term "dueling" correctly because from my research, most of the stick fights in the Philippines had rules (even if only tacitly agreed upon) such as having a second in the space, when a fight was over, restrictions and so on. Remy participated in a number of these when he was a kid and young man. He even told his balintawak eskrima teacher, Anciong Bacon, that he was not going to teach stick fighting but *"for sport…and for self-defense, not fighting."*

And that is what he taught, self-defense and mostly the art. However, he would often inject *"But in real…"* and demonstrate the technique he was doing in a simpler and more deadly fashion. He would usually come back to the safer version of the move he was showing but the astute student would make a note of the real deal action.

"But first you must go slow."

Yeah, right! When teaching any technique or drill, Prof. Remy would turn into "Hollywood Remy." He would do the action fast and strong… repeatedly. Often I was on the receiving end of these demonstrations. You had to really pay attention to what the heck he was doing in order to get it. He then, in the middle of his fast demonstrations, would say *"But first you must go slow."* and then he would smile broadly and then ramp it up again. It got to a point where I would chuckle to myself when he said that because he seldom ever demonstrated anything slowly.

But he did have a point. I think I must be one of the last people to hear this particular phrase, "slow is smooth and smooth is fast." I first heard that from Bruce Chiu, another long time student of Prof. Remy's and this made total sense. You initially go slow so that you can make the sense of the separate parts of the technique. From there you connect the separate parts so that you can go from one to the next smoothly. Once you have smooth down, you can increase the speed. *"But first you must go slow."*

* *Modern Arnis - The Martial Art of Remy Presas pg. 19*

"This is why the art is so beautiful. There are so many things you can do."

Again, this one dealt with options. I look at it as option transitions. One set up can lead anywhere. From one setup you can go into a joint lock, a throw, a disarm, a simple counter strike – anything! This is so simple yet so profound. THIS is the reason why he taught us so many techniques; to give us the skillset to recognize and apply many options. Sweet!

A humorous look at this aphorism is that Prof. Remy would often immobilize me in a joint lock. I would be tapping away and he would keep talking and talking and talking to the crowd. Thanks to Photoshop...(come on, you gotta have a sense of humor).

"If you can counter the counter, nobody will beat you."

Prof. Remy related to different students in different ways. I was a well-known karate fighter when we met. I was a US national Top Ten rated fighter at the time so he would often relate to me from a fighter's viewpoint. I remember one time we were in casual conversation when he turned serious and said to me, *"Danny, if you can counter the counter, you will not be beaten."* Unlike some of his other aphorisms, this one made sense to me right away and has been a guiding light, a pillar of my own Modern Arnis training ever since. This, to me, is so important that it is something I work on all the time so that I can never be caught off guard.

I have a funny story regarding this. I was teaching at the 2021 Modern Arnis Legacy Camp and my partner was Roland Rivera. Roland is a highly skilled Modern Arnis player in his own right and a very playful guy. I was demonstrating a counter the counter concept while talking to the attendees and he did an unexpected move. Mid action (and mid my yakking) he stepped behind me for a diving throw position. Off the cuff, I countered him with a back scoop kick to the groin. This wasn't planned. This was an immediate option. This sequence of events was all within a second. This is the split-second option recognition that came out of the   aphorism *"If you can counter the counter, nobody will beat you."*

PS - What I don't show you is him getting me off balance right after the kick. Hey - it's my book after all.)

"You must have the flow."

I will go over the Flow in depth in the section called *Technical Pillars of Modern Arnis* but there is a song written by the great Duke Ellington with a lyric that says it all – *"It don't mean a thing if it ain't got that swing."* Well, if it ain't got the Flow, it's not Modern Arnis.

Remy

You've probably noticed by now that I ever refer to Prof. Remy by just his first name. It's always "Professor" or "Prof. Remy." With my senior -junior ethic firmly in place, I was boringly stiff around him. I remember numerous times Prof. Remy saying to me, "Danny, call me Remy." I'd answer "Yes, sir...Professor." If I had any regrets is that I didn't let him in close enough to me. Oh, well.

One of the things in martial arts is that it is easy to deify your instructor to the point where you never really see the person. I was like that with Prof. Remy. One thing that I did see, however, was that he liked to laugh...a lot. Here was this technical marvel and fierce warrior yucking it up. Since I was so stiff around him, I don't really have any funny Professor stories but others do. Here are a couple for you on the next page.

Remy Presas as the Karate Kid

Remy

You've probably noticed by now that I ever refer to Prof. Remy by just his first name. It's always "Professor" or "Prof. Remy." With my senior-junior ethic firmly in place, I was boringly stiff around him. I remember numerous times Prof. Remy saying to me, *"Danny, call me Remy."* I'd answer *"Yes, sir...Professor."* If I had any regrets is that I didn't let him in close enough to me. Oh, well.

One of the things in martial arts is that it is easy to deify your instructor to the point where you never really see the person. I was like that with Prof. Remy. One thing that I did see, however, was that he liked to laugh...a lot. Here was this technical marvel and fierce warrior yucking it up. Since I was so stiff around him, I don't really have any funny Professor stories but others do. Here are several for you.

Brian Zawilinski: Larry Rocha and I were training in a park in Victoria, B.C. Professor waited until a couple to walk by. When they did, he threw his hand while bowing his head down and yelped *"No! No! Don't hurt me!"*

Bruce Chiu: Driving him in LA. Car cuts us off.
RP: *"Why did you let that happen? You must give them the sign!!!!!"*
Me: *"What sign, what are talking about?"*
RP: *"Catch up to them."*
I catch up and pull alongside on their left side. He leans out the window so his entire upper body is out of the car and starts flipping them off. He comes back in and looks at me and says *"That is the sign!"*

Frank Shekosky: When Professor found out I was engaged he said that's very smart and I will be very happy. It's good to get married. Several feet away he then spoke with a student of mine who said he had no current plan to get married. Professor said *"That is smart. Don't get married. Getting married is bad."*

Tim Gustavson: As his young uke for two days my joints had about had it. He then gets excited with a center lock. I dropped, or dove if you will, knee first trying to get in front of the direction of the pain. Yet,

unintentionally, delivering a full weight knee slam to his bare foot. He continued to pin me to the ground per usual showing little sign of the blow. Break is called and during this time, Lynn Anderson is chatting with RP, she walks over to confide what he said, *"That Team. Team is barrry heavy."* (Note: Tim his replicating his accent. DA) After the break he's demoing with tennis shoes on now. I'm hiding in the back. About 15 minutes go by, he gets extra animated, smiling and shouts: *"Where is Team, Team where are you?"* I jump up and say, *"Here Sir!" "There is Team. Now Team funch me, funch me hard!"* I do as commanded and end up in a standing center lock this time. RP pushes my arm up high making me dance on my tip toes, as he steps under my arm to cement the lock further, a courtesy foot stomp with a twisting grind to my bare foot…
"The standing center lock"

Peter Hobart: New England Summer Camp in the Mid-Nineties (both time and temperature). Chris Pedrick and I had been cracking rattan sticks against each other for several hours, to the point that you could smell--and almost see--the smoke. In a moment of sweaty distraction, I felt the index finger of my stick-hand getting pinched between my weapon's grip and his. The pain was exquisite and rapidly accelerating, and the only escape path I could find involved swinging the punyo in a rapid downward arc. Unfortunately, this caused it to come to rest somewhere in the region of Chris's groin…

Now this particular Summer Camp was always held on a college campus, and sessions usually ran late into the evening, so students often spent the night in empty dorm rooms and shared meals in the school's cafeteria. So it was the next morning that Chris and I were sitting together at the breakfast table when the Professor stopped by the check in. Seeing my bandaged index finger, he said [and please forgive the substitution of "p" for "f" and vice versa--I want you to hear this exchange in his voice]:

RP: *"Feter! What happen to you pinger?"*
PH: *"Sir, Chris rudely hit me with his cane yesterday."*
RP: *"Chris, is it true!?"*
CP: *"Yes, but in fairness, I should add that Peter then immediately hit me back in the groin."*

RP: [After mulling it over for a second] *"Well Chris, in that case, you are the loser!"*

Chad Bailey: There were many times he would have me in a lock and would say to the group as they were joking, *"See... Chad is not laughing!"*

Well, maybe a slight smile.

It is easy to forget what a character he was. No matter how high of a pedestal we put him on, he was very human. And he could be very funny.

Technical Pillars of Modern Arnis

This section is longer than my usual essays and deserves a chapter of its own.

There are techniques and there are principles and concepts. You can get techniques from anywhere but without an underlying foundation, they remain just techniques. How do you master an art? How do you advance your own skills? What has worked for me is to delve into the foundational concepts and principles of said art. Robert W. Smith, noted author of many martial arts books (one of my favorite martial arts authors, by the way), said in a book review, *"Teach me the principle and I can create a thousand techniques."* That is how I operate. Show me the principle. Teach me the concept and I'll go from there.

Remy Presas did not teach in a scientific manner. He threw tons and tons of techniques drills at us. Some were connected and some were stand-alone actions. He would use aphorisms (*def. an observation that contains a general truth, such as, "if it ain't broke, don't fix it."*) to back up something he taught but very little in the way of concrete principles or concepts. That drove me nuts so I decided to use my martial arts knowledge and experience to dig into the art to come up with the principles of is. The results of this research are what I call the *Technical Pillars of Modern Arnis*.

Much of what follows is based on observation, both visual and tactile, of how Prof. Remy moved and cross referencing it with what I have trained in and studied in other martial arts. You will read lots that you never heard Prof. Remy say himself.

Again, my observations in my own words. Some of these topics I will go in depth on. Other points I will remark on briefly. And remember one thing – this is from a *Dan perspective*.

Angles Of Attack

Filipino martial arts have one particular distinction that makes them different than most every other one. They do not name their strikes. They number them. Coming from a karate background, I found this fascinating. I was used to the terms straight punch, knife hand strike, spinning hook kick and the like. Right off the bat, Prof. Remy taught us "number 1," "number 2" and so forth. The twelve strikes in Modern Arnis were taught as the twelve angles of attack. At the time this was fascinating but over time it made sense. Let me explain.

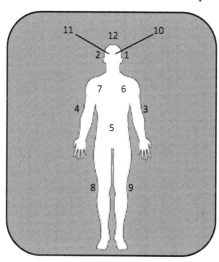

Styles Of Arnis

In most martial arts, we are taught a particular "style." Examples of this are karate types like Shotokan, Goju-ryu and so on. Takewondo is considered a Korean style. Wing Chun is looked at a style of Kung Fu. And so on. Well, if you look at the definition of the word itself, using the term "style" is a bit of a misnomer regarding martial arts types.

Style definition: a manner of doing something. *"different styles of management"*

When the Japanese and Korean pioneers began to disseminate karate and taekwondo, English was their second language. Term *ryu* was used by many practitioners to describe their type of karate.

Ryu definition: Ryū mainly used as a suffix, meaning style, type, form, manner, system, school, used here in the sense of ryūha (*a school or a school of thought*) is the Japanese term referring to a *school* in any discipline. The kanji itself is commonly used as a suffix (from Google translations, italics mine).

The pioneers used the term "style" and it stuck. Let's look at the word "style" from a Filipino martial art concept. The term "classical styles" is used a lot in FMA. These are different movement patterns of the stick (or blade) itself and when coupled with the 12 angles of attack, they cover not only every angle an attack can come at your form but also every manner of their delivery method as well. Add all this up and you train yourself to develop spontaneous recognition.

So, what are the classical styles contained within Modern Arnis? You have:

- banda y banda (side by side)
- rompida (vertical up and down slashing)
- figure 8 (upward angular slashing both forehand and backhand)
- reverse figure 8 (downward angular slashing both forehand and backhand)
- abaniko (a speed strike using the wrist action to deliver it)
- redonda (a single or double stick circular vertical striking method)

- sinawali (a double stick weaving pattern containing multiple strikes)

Now consider this. Throw them all into the mixing bowl. Combine them all into any random series and you have what I call a machine gun attack. Drill them all and you develop a supreme ability to recognize any attack coming at you from any direction. I always wondered why Prof. Remy was never surprised when we changed up on him during training. He was so familiar with motion that he always saw it coming.

I'm always surprised when the *styles of arnis* get a bit of a short shrift with some Modern Arnis players. They, in my opinion, form a larger part of the overall make-up of Modern Arnis than many people suspect. Add these to the angles of attack and you have movement of the stick from all directions as well as manners of striking.

Angling/Body Shifting
This is one of the first taught, most important, and unfortunately, frequently neglected actions by Modern Arnis players. Most Modern Arnis players use angling/body shifting for these two purposes:
- To reposition the target so that it does not get hit or
- To reposition the target so that if it does get hit, the degree of impact will be lessened.

Let's take a look at this before I get on to what I use angling and body shifting for.

In defensive stepping, the first thing to understand is that the attacker is going to hit at what is there. They are going to hit at a target. The target is located in a very exact position in space. So, you remove the target from that exact location. A good example is using an angle step as part of your defense against a #1 strike. Your left temple is the target. Your opponent strikes at it so you remove it from the trajectory of the strike. This is simple.

You can also use angling/ body shifting to lessen the impact of the oncoming strike. Let's go back to the attacker for a moment. They are hitting at something, a target. They will strike in such a manner so that the strike will hit with the strongest degree of impact. I'm not only talking about a trained attacker but an untrained one also. A good analogy is baseball. The batter times his swing to meet the ball at maximum impact. If he swings too soon or too late, he won't get a good piece of the ball. The impact will be less. This is the idea of purpose 2.

You can diminish the degree of impact of the stick by either moving in towards the strike before it has a lot of power generated or by moving away from the power of the strike and catching it as it weakens. Moving into it isn't one of the smartest things to do but it is better than getting hit full force by it. If you use a cane to block or brace, then it will be a little safer to move into the strike. You move to a point either before or after the attacker's desired point of impact, where it will have less force if it connects.

I use angling/body shifting for an entirely different purpose. I use it to achieve superior positioning and alignment (Note: I'll add more on this subject under its own heading later in this chapter).

Being first a karate practitioner I look at having four weapons at my disposal; two arms and two legs. When i face off at my opponent or training partner, generally he or she is facing me with four weapons at their disposal as well. I want to unbalance that equation in my favor. I do this by angle stepping. When I step off the line of fire, I reposition myself so that I still have four weapons at my disposal but they have less at theirs. That is why I step. Getting out of the way of an attack is a convenient byproduct of angle stepping, in my view, but it is not the prime reason I step. I want offensive and defensive positional superiority even if only for a split second.

Prof. Remy stressed the importance of angling in the first sense (defensive stepping) back in the initial days of my instruction from him. I already did that in karate competition against fighters who rushed headlong at me but I never really thought about it much beyond that one application – get off the railroad tracks before the train ran you down. It wasn't until I put a weapon in my hand that I began looking at angling and body shifting in a different light. Positional and alignment superiority became a more important reason to angle than just defensive stepping.

There is another reason why I don't use angling/body shifting to "get out of the way of an attack." To me, this is fighting with one foot going out the back door. Mentally it is working from an effect viewpoint rather than one of being cause. What do I mean by effect viewpoint? *"Oy! He's coming at me! I've got to do something quick to get out of the way!"* Yikes! Reaction. Defensive. Being the negative effect of his action. That is an *effect* viewpoint. So, what is a cause viewpoint. It is simply doing an action because you want to. "Here he comes. I think I'll move over there." That is a *cause* viewpoint. Yes, your opponent is moving first. Yes, you are stepping off the line of attack. What is different between the two. Attitude. Are you getting the hell out of Dodge or going over here because you like the view better? The difference in attitude makes all the difference in the world.

Let's look at a much neglected use of angling/body shifting, offensive use.

Angling as you strike you will put yourself out of your opponent's optimum line of return striking. Your strike will be stronger if you use some sort of body torque or rotation with the strike than if you just swing with the arm alone.

One last point before I move on, mobility plays a very big part in angling and body shifting. To be mobile you need to be prepared to move. This is where practitioners screw up big time. They aren't prepared to move. With my students I will refer to this as "the lazy American." We live in a culture where we sit on chairs, sofas, recliners, stools and the like. We don't squat. We aren't used to bending our knees to any great degree. We have a tendency to stand with our legs relatively straight. If you stand with your legs relatively straight, your first action will be to bend your knees instead of just move. This is a secret hidden factor to "bad timing." I'll get to that later.

When your knees are bent, you can spring immediately. If they aren't, they'll need to bend first and then spring. This bending action of the knees will waste a split instant of time - and that's all it takes to get hit with a stick. When your opponent attacks or when you spot their telegraph of motion, you want to move instantly, prepare to move and then move. Be prepared to move by having your knees bent and you will be able to move instantly rather than slightly late.

Footwork is a key aspect to Modern Arnis. If you see videos or films of Professor Presas sometime when he isn't demonstrating for beginners but actually moving with someone, you'll notice his knees are bent and he is ready to go. He moves without delay and is never caught off balance. Work this into your training, having your knees bent. Be ready to move.

The Check Hand

Ahhhh, the check hand. The use of the hand that is not holding the weapon is of prime importance. Guro Dan Inosanto calls this the "live hand." My teacher in balintawak eskrima, Ted Buot, called it "the quarterback." This should give the importance of it. To emphasize its importance, Prof. Remy would tell me, *"Danny, do not be hypnotized by the stick."* This would come from my utter fascination of what one could do with the stick that in the beginning, my check hand would not do much of anything. With beginners, when they put a weapon in their hand, it seems that all of their attention goes on that weapon and their other hand is often dangling at their side, useless and forgotten.

Prof. Remy was very adept at grabbing his opponent's cane. GM Cristino Vasquez called it the secret of Modern Arnis. Generally speaking, grabbing the stick is generally frowned upon by other FMA players. Some will say that the stick represents the blade and you'd never grab the blade. Well, the stick is not the blade. I train totally differently when I have a blade in my hand than when I have a stick.

Others will say to not chase the stick. And again many will say it is too fast to grab and if you catch it in mid strike, you'll get your hand broken. There is nothing wrong with any of these reasons but speaking for myself, grabbing the cane is one of the options for check hand usage. The timing of this is especially crucial…if you don't know what you are doing. Datu Dieter Knuttel has a way of setting up the grab so that one can learn it quickly and effectively. Rather than using the check hand to brace the stick from the oncoming blow, the check hand rides the with the stick and then snatches your opponent's cane in a single move.

Hand is in a position so that your little fingers can reach behind your cane.

Hand is in a position so that your little fingers can reach in front of your cane.

The key to the snatch is the position of your check hand. Note that in the top two photos that my little fingers are slightly behind my cane. This makes it easy to grab his cane and counter strike on a highline. In the bottom two photos, my hand is angled so that my little fingers have access to his cane at a point in front of my cane. This sets me up for a low line counter strike.

From Manong Ted Buot, I learned other usages of the check hand; to manage, maneuver and delay your opponent's stick. Karate wise, I already knew one of my favorite uses of the check hand – to punch my opponent. Both Prof. Remy and GM Bobby Taboada use the left hand as a sharp, jolting strike/push. Prof. Remy called this "tusok" (thrust). Yep, don't be hypnotized by the stick.

Reality In Training
Back in the Philippines reality in training was never much of a problem. If you missed a block, you got hit. You miss too many of them or miss even just one hard strike you got injured. The necessity level of the trainee rose in proportion to the amount of danger in the training. You either got good, got crippled, or got out.

When Prof. Remy was a kid, this is how he was taught. His father, Jose, taught the Filipino guerrillas in World War ll. This was not sport or art. It was real deal, live or die application training. Young Remy was trained by his grandfather, Leon, in real deal stick fighting. Unfortunately, arnis and eskrima had a bad reputation. It was the fighting of street thugs, dock workers and various low life. Prof. Presas saw that Arnis was becoming a dying art for just that reason. Imported martial arts were much more popular. Karate, Judo and Taekwondo were "civilized." They had schools, orderly training, uniforms and the like. Like the song by XTC, *"No Thugs In Our House."*

Prof. Remy changed that when he taught in the school system. He formulated a curriculum, had the students wear uniforms, did unison training in groups – all the civilized things that karate and the like did. He even had the students strike the sticks instead of arms and knuckles as defensive actions. He carried these aspects over when he came to the United States.

"Safety first" was his teaching motto.

Unfortunately, I have seen it go too far in the U.S. From the people I have seen, when a student is striking to the arm for example, in the name of safety the strike ends up about 6 inches from even touching the arm. That is nice but much of what the Professor learned he learned the hard way - in actual fights against a real opponent who wanted to hurt him. So, a lot of the defenses are against real attacks, not strikes that stop a foot away.

The way that I stress is what Manong Ted taught to do. He would have me hold the stick at a right angle to my grip, with no flex or play in the wrist. This way I be exactly on target and could stop my strike an inch from hitting my partner's head or tag lightly any other target. He called this "No room for discussion." Love it. Now, no more swinging over the top of a partner's head and saying "If I was really hitting for your head..." nonsense. In closing, something I tell my students – *"I don't train myself to miss...ever!"*

Centering

This is an interesting one as far as Modern Arnis is concerned. Because there are no "fixed position" stances in Modern Arnis as there are in the forms of Karate, Kung Fu, and so forth, one can get into the idea that stances are not needed in Modern Arnis. Add to that the fact that Prof. Remy never said *"You must stand this way..."* when teaching. He would outline them in his books but the subject never really came up when he was teaching on the floor.

To a point, this idea is correct. One doesn't use stop-freeze-set positions in Modern Arnis applications. So what is the deal with the stances then? Let's take a look at what the various stances mean to teach: to be *centered* (balanced) in whatever positions your feet end up in.

Being centered means that your upper body is not extended too far in any direction from a straight up and down alignment with your hips so that you maintain balance. Your knees are bent and your hips are lowered. Whoa. This is almost taiji like!

Why do I bring this up? Because you seldom caught Prof. Remy off-balance. Interesting. Off the top of my head I don't recall him going off-balance. Why was this? Because he never got his structure out of alignment. So, what's the importance of structure and alignment? Coming up next.

Structure

Structure has to do with posture, balance, and natural body positioning. Another way to put it is Structure is the manner of positioning the body so that the muscles, tendons and ligaments are in natural alignment. Structure and alignment are looked at as the same thing but I make the distinction with structure having to do with the natural position of the body while alignment has to do with your positioning in relation to your opponent's. In a sense they are 'twin brothers' yet, for me, they are their own separate subjects. When I look at structure I look at the structural alignment body itself, structural alignment.

The human body is designed to be upright.

If you look at standing structure you will find that the bones align in a vertical manner, up and down. This is such a simplicity that it is often overlooked. Your posture is often stressed when you are growing up. Do you remember mom or dad telling you *"Stand up straight. Don't slouch. Lift your shoulders up."* I sure do. When I trained in baguazhang I found that structure/posture is highly emphasized. Structure is essential as it has to do with your equilibrium, a fancy way of saying keeping your balance. It has to do with power development. It has to do with practically every element of core essentials, it is that important.

Here is something for you to think with - your key to superior position or structure is to maintain *your* structure while breaking your opponent's. Look at the photo of Prof. Remy on the preceding page.

In taking a look at structure a very key point is to keep the spinal column vertical. It is easy to do this. All you need to do is to tuck your butt under your waist. This is something that has been overlooked by many Modern Arnis practitioners as it is not very exciting or dramatic looking. I suppose it lacks an esthetic flair. It has everything to do with balance in combat, however.

Phillip Starr's book, *Martial Mechanics*, and Steven Perlman's book, *The Book Of Martial Power*, both stress the need for proper structure as well as good spinal alignment. Perlman states, *"Arguably, this is the single most overlooked principle of martial arts."* I whole heartedly agree. Starr makes a good point when he states, *"In order to unify your upper and lower body so that you can move powerfully from your dantien you must maintain proper alignment of the spinal column. The dantien (in Japanese, the tanden) is located roughly three finger-widths below the navel and about two finger-widths inside."* What I bring your attention is where he states *"in order to unify your body..."*

Structure (along with alignment) has a lot to do with the transfer of power to your opponent when you connect with your strike as well. When I strike I rotate my hips for power. Rotating from the hips will maintain spinal alignment. I emphasize this so that the spine will not become twisted. The spine will naturally twist to some degree but I like to not push it. Your muscles, tendons and ligaments will prevent the spine from over rotating.

A key to keeping your balance is to maintain your structure while striking. This means using your footwork to cover the necessary distance to your opponent rather than attempting to hit him by overreaching.

Alignment
Where I draw the line between structure and alignment is that structure has to do with balance and the natural up & down position of the body. Alignment has to do with your position in relation to your opponent for maximum efficiency in your application of techniques.

You can have beautiful structure and be out of alignment. Your alignment can be perfect but your structure can be off. I call them the twin brothers; one should not exist without the other. Again, alignment is your position relative to your opponent's position. When you are squared off with your opponent you are on what I call the "Connection Line." You and your opponent are faced off, in good alignment, at each other. You are, in a sense, connected.

Here is a 'Dan-ism.' When you are in good alignment with your opponent, you are in basically a position to execute a boxing jab/cross combination. This position is what I find best to set you up for both cane and check hand usage. Here is where you are aligned for maximum weapons usage. The jab-cross positioning ensures you have all your weapons where you can use them. Unless engaged in a joint lock or body manipulation which calls for a different body set up, the jab/cross position is your alignment to your opponent. The photos on the next page show exactly what I mean.

This set of photos is from my book *Filipino Martial Arts* and shows my alignment from a head on position. No matter how I angle I keep the same jab-cross alignment with my opponent when I move.

As outlined earlier in this text, angle stepping is one of the signature actions of Modern Arnis. Let's get a bit more specific on how the two interrelate. When you angle step, your distance alignment (how close or far you are away from your opponent and your alignment for that distance) is going to be different for different actions. Your block and counter strike degree of angle will be larger than your angle to execute a disarm technique. Your block and counter lock or throw degree of angle will be sharper than your disarm angle. I call this "shaving the angle." One of the finer points of alignment is knowing how sharp to cut the angle in order to execute any particular move. It is even more important to understand what you *cannot* execute from which degree of angle. These are fine points of alignment that can be taught and understood.

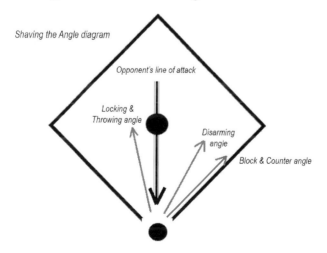

Zoning is another alignment factor. Zoning, simply stated, is the action of going from the line of fire to a safe spot. Example: strike number 1 (forehand strike to the head or temple). The line of fire is from the chamber spot to the point of contact. This is the space the cane travels through. This is a hot zone. Moving to the side where the cane is not traveling through is called zoning. I call the safe space the dead zone. Whether you step or lean, you are still zoning.

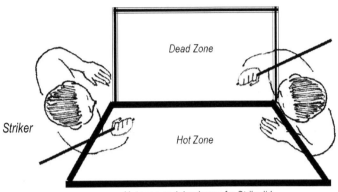

Hot zone and dead zone for Strike #1

Note: You won't always make the 'right' decision and will sometimes move into the hot zone. This is not necessarily a problem when you understand one thing and that is the designated point of impact. When a person is striking at another with an impact weapon, they will deliver the strike to hit the hardest when it reaches the target. Any untrained person will do this naturally. The fascinating thing is that, like moving your finger past a flame and not getting burned, when you move into the strike, you are moving into the hot zone before it becomes really hot. You jam the strike before it gains decent impact power. Even though this is a "mistake," this is a drill point that is often overlooked. You should drill this until "accidentally moving into the strike" is as correct as zoning out of the path.

Structure During Transition
Hah! This is almost never talked about yet it is incredibly important! These next two sections are very important, but overlooked parts in martial arts teaching. These are:
    1.How to maintain your structure while moving and
    2.How to maintain your alignment while moving.

Structure in transition has to do with not letting the body go out of structure and alignment *while in motion*. This is the toughest thing to do in either solo exercises or partner training.

If you look at the construct of any cycle of action, it is composed of three aspects:

- start,
- change and
- stop.

It is relatively easy to have structure while you are at the beginning of a move or after you are done moving. Start from not moving and stopping after you are done is easy. It is in the aspect of change where this becomes difficult. This requires incredible command of the body.

This is something that is not talked about very much. When you go from one position to another, a lot of emphasis is placed on the finish or stop position. Your transitioning is equally important if not even more important than the finish position. Structure and balance in movement takes lot of practice and work.

Faulty structure in transition is hardly ever spoken about yet it is one of the prime reasons your locking or throwing fails. I have seen where a student will successfully break his partner's structure, be in proper alignment and yet then go off balance or fail to execute successfully. Then he tries again with the same result. After a while he either gives up the move as incomprehensible or reverts to the time honored solution beginners use – go faster and harder. What is hardly ever spotted is that his own structure was broken by his own action and that is what caused the technique to fail. Well, how do we develop this?

Anyo (forms) training is perfect for developing structure in transition. Quite often forms stress going from structure to structure with the emphasis being the final position you land in. You can see this in practically any karate competition. From pose to pose the form looks great. What is more important is the maintenance of your structure during your movement. The more your body falls out of structure during movement, the less likely you will be able to execute your action. It is not necessary to stiffen your body in an attempt to maintain structure.

Concentration on moving your body *as an entire unit* is going to be the key.

This was really brought to my attention was when I began training in baguazhang. The stepping was slow and the emphasis was connection with my entire body. A great way to solo train this aspect is to do the arnis forms slowly using the taiji heel-toe, 'single weighting' type of step. It will be frustrating for you at first but the benefits are many fold.

Another way to train maintaining your structure and breaking your partner's structure is to develop a willingness *to occupy your partner's space* – to occupy his space, not just coexist in it. This is an unseen point where most locking actions and throws fail.

Quite often I've seen a student try a lock or throw on their partner yet unconsciously avoid bumping into their partner. They'll bend their body or not get close and so forth. This keeps you from keeping your structural integrity intact. The ability to do this is a must for self-defense abilities. If you freeze when your opponent gets too close to you he will have the advantage.

Why should there be such an emphasis on maintaining structure in transition? Simple. When you begin to manipulate your opponent you will need all the balance you can get to execute your technique successfully. Any opponent who has any experience will attempt to counter you during your transition. If your structure is maintained during movement or action, you will be in a stronger position to reverse their action.

Another thing to consider is that your opponent might try to feint you out of position in order to execute his technique. Out of position is another way of saying out of structure. However under-stressed this is, one of the most important core basics in Modern Arnis.

Alignment During Transition

This is a blood brother to structure in transition. Simply stated this is keeping your position or alignment while you move. The first way I teach this is when executing block and counter exercises. While you angle step and block, work on maintaining your jab/cross alignment.

Another good way to practice this is first to keep visual alignment with your partner as you train. This is another "no-brainer" as it is dangerous to take your eyes off your opponent but many people do. When you take your eyes off of your opponent it is too easy for you to misalign yourself and you are liable to their counter to your action. You do not need to stare at him to do this. Keeping him in your peripheral vision is just fine. The main thing is to not lose awareness of your opponent while executing a move.

The key is preferably to never go out of optimum alignment with your opponent while keeping your opponent out of alignment with you. Maintaining alignment while in motion is a key to superiority.

One thing I remember about working with Prof. Remy was it was so hard to get him out of position. Part of the problem was he was very adept at getting me out of position while keeping his. He did this whether he moved or stood still. This is another discovery I made by observing him and feeling him execute on me.

Arm Sensitivity

This is a topic usually discussed in amazement at how Prof. Remy's sensitivity was so good for someone so strong. Usually strong people just go Neanderthal on you and rip you limb from limb. Prof. Remy didn't. He felt and guided you into his next action. He was as sensitive as any taiji player I have met. He was scary sensitive.

Okay. Prof. Remy could do this but how about the rest of us mere mortals? How do we develop this sensitivity? Well, after doing many, many stick and empty hand flow drills it all boils down to one simple point:

Pay attention to your partner.

There you go. That's the secret. I know. The first question usually asked is "What do you mean by that?" It is too simple but here goes. Pay attention to your partner. Pay attention to what *he does* when he is executing any technique on you. Most people put great concentration on how to do a technique when they are the ones applying it. I step here, I move your arm there – that sort of thing. Then when it's their partner's turn to practice repetitions, they'll think of the last presidential election, what the Kardashians are up to, why the IRS is auditing them and so forth. Then when it's their turn again, they concentrate on the technique again. They are missing the important part of the training; paying attention to how their body feels when their partner is executing on them.

An example: Your partner is practicing a two-hand wrist lock on you. They grab your hand. Their thumb is on the back of your hand and their fingers are in your palm. They rotate your wrist outward and bend it at the same time. At some point in the execution it hurts like hell. If you pay attention, the first thing you will feel is something small touching the back of your hand while more is touching your palm. Then you will feel your hand moving in a semi-circle towards your shoulder or ribs. Then you'll feel the pain. Close your eyes and have your partner execute (slowly) a two-hand wrist lock on you and you will note this sequence I described. That is the paying attention part. Next is the frosting on the cake.

You'll have to turn the page for this.

A joint lock or throw is a precision action. If you ruin the precision, you ruin the action. With the two-hand wrist lock you will notice that it travels in a semi-circular motion until it hits a point where pain turns on. So, what do you do to counter it? Simple.

1. Contribute to the motion (not fight it) and
2. Change the trajectory.

You do this and your hand won't end up in the position that causes the pain. You develop sensitivity by paying attention to your partner's action, the entire thing, every step along the way. After doing this with many, many techniques you will feel where your partner wants to go without having to look. One of my favorite things to do at seminars is to call out for volunteers to joint lock me. Then I will apply the above to foil the lock. I will even tell them that I am going to close my eyes to make it easier for them. In over 20 years, nobody has joint locked me yet.

Offensively, I teach and train what I call blind locking and blind trapping. Blind locking (and trapping) goes like this: I strike at my partner and he blocks. I go by feel and take the blocking motion he made and transform it into a joint lock. I then let up on the lock and strike again. My partner blocks and I take the motion and lock him again. And so on. With blind trapping I use his blocking or parrying action and transform it into a trapping action on and on and on.

An exercise Prof. Presas stressed was called flowing locks. This is where you transferred from one joint lock to another to another. You could use this to follow your opponent's resistance, to move him from one position to another or put you into a better position yourself. This exercise teaches not only arm sensitivity but facility with the locks as well.

I don't know how Prof. Remy got so sensitive but he above is how I replicate his skill for myself and others.

Incorporate A Curve

I trained ever so briefly in the Chinese martial art of Baguazhang. I have always been fascinated by an art which utilizes so many circles instead of straight line applications. After training in this art I noticed something about the Professor. About 95% or his actions, whether stepping, locking, disarming and so forth, all incorporate a curve of some sort. He never mentioned anything to me about this but in observing him, I saw that he uses circular actions, but the word circular is a little deceiving. It may mean to some that he moves in a circle. Incorporating a curve says it better. There is a fascinating absence of straight lines in many things that he does.

Timing

Everybody has it. Nobody can easily define it. Everyone complains about having trouble with it but they demonstrate it expertly in everyday living. Timing...the great conundrum.

For me, timing is simple. Timing is a *decision of when*. When what? When anything. There is no mystical secret to timing. Everything you do in life has timing involved. If you have a forkful of food and stick yourself in the mouth with the fork, your timing was off. The mouth didn't open soon enough or you closed it too soon. Timing is everywhere in life, so much so that it is taken for granted.

Timing is a decision of when. That's all. If your timing is off, you're either too soon or too late. That's all there is to it.

Well, there's one more thing and it's what I call the "hidden bitch." Lack of preparation will give the apparancy of poor timing. You can have perfect timing but waste that split instant, using it to go from unprepared to prepared. Example: You see an opening in your opponent's defense. This is the right time to go forward at him but your knees aren't bent. You end up using that exact split instant to bend your knees instead of springing forward. You get there late. You wasted your perfect point of timing by using that pinpoint split instant to get ready rather than being ready in the first place.

You can offset that one by being ready in the first place.

Distancing

Against an inexperienced stick fighter the best ranges to be at are either out of stick hitting range or inside swinging range. That can't be said, however, for an experienced Modern Arnis player or eskrimador. An experienced player can change from a stick swing to a tip or butt poke to an empty hand strike and so forth depending on the circumstances. Distancing here applies to knowing exactly what you can do from how far away or close in you are. When you know that it is better to use the butt of the cane to strike from close in and swing from far away, you can then predict and neutralize your opponent by knowing what he can do also.

Use a cane against a heavy bag or a tree to find out for yourself what your exact distance has to be for a full cane swing, a backhand/forehand flick (abaniko), poke, butt strike and others. You can experiment with power striking on these. Then work on finding those ranges with a partner. Then work on predicting your partner's range with those strikes against you. Work with partners of different sizes and reaches and you will find yourself becoming proficient in using distancing to attack and defend with.

Translation

This is the translation of cane actions to empty hand or other weapons and vice versa. Example: the up stroke in a figure 8 strike can also be used as an uppercut punch, knife slash, standing center lock, backward throw to name a few. An interesting thing to note is in traditional Arnis and eskrima, a student is first taught how to use a cane and later the empty hand. In Modern Arnis, the cane actions are the punches and the locking and the throwing. They are interchangeable.

83

Two Way Action

You will notice that in doing any kind of disarm or lock, if you apply two directions of force the action will be much more effective. The directions are usually either in opposing directions or in an ever tightening circle.

The two way action of Prof. Presas' joint locking techniques came directly from Prof. Wally Jay, founder of Small Circle Jujutsu. He and Prof. Jay were "road buddies" for 15 years. They did many seminars together and were joined later by George Dillman, the Ryukyu Kenpo pressure point expert and put on many "Big Three" seminars. Over the years I watched (and painfully felt) the influence Prof. Jay had on Prof. Presas' joint locking techniques. Prof. Presas went from big flowing circular moves to very small, immediately painful moves.

Making The Connection

In Modern Arnis making the connection is the ability to recognize the possibilities of what you can do from any given position. We all heard the Professor saying *"When you can do this you will be able to make the connection."* Making the connection is the ability to recognize the possibilities of where you can go from where you are. This point is so valid that it is important to note that Datu Kelly Worden (below middle) used Modern Arnis to make the connection to every other martial art he had previously learned.

When you first start your training, you are taught techniques and patterns. It's easy to take the proscribed techniques and patterns as *the* way to do it. However, once you get good enough at the patterns and so forth you begin to see the possibilities and that's where making the connection begins. The wrist lock doesn't only lead into the arm bar but into the finger lock or head throw or the takedown as well. From that point you begin to see some (and later all) of the possibilities and more importantly, you begin to work off your opponent's reactions. This is definitely above rote applications and patterns but it's getting down the techniques and patterns so well that will allow you to step out of the patterns, etc.

So what are we looking at? The more you train, the more tools you develop. The more tools you develop, the more tools you have in your toolbox. The more tools you have in your toolbox, the more options you have at your disposal. Now, to add to that, this is how I view it. If you have practiced enough, a tool will pop out when appropriate. This is something I have *experienced* over and over again. You and your partner are in a position and he plays screw your buddy. Bing! Something pops out of the toolbox which appropriately handles the action.

Here is where recognition comes into play. I tell my students all the time "Recognition is senior to analytical thought." If you practice many, many techniques, many, many approaches, in time you will recognize them all faster than an eyeblink. And at the same time you will respond (note: NOT "react" - to me, reaction is robotic and not in present time) appropriately. To me, this is a vital aspect to the flow which I gained from both my fighting career and Modern Arnis from Remy Presas.

Here's an additional thing to ponder. The various drills in Modern Arnis not only develop coordination but they expand beyond that to develop recognition. Split second recognition opens the door to spontaneity in using what you have from your tool box.

As you can see, there are no limits to where you can go from any action. This is why I teach my students a wide variety of actions rather than a limited number. This corresponds with the viewpoint of the system I use for teaching karate. I call it the 3 stages of understanding the martial arts.

- Stage 1 is learning the technique. This is going through the move and getting it correctly.
- Stage 2 is duplicating the technique. This is getting a full understanding of the action conceptually and an ability to perform it correctly.

- Stage 3 is creating the technique based on a full understanding of the action. At Stage 3 you are now able to create other actions off of that understanding.

Prof. Presas would say, *"You can do that, too."* You see what he means? At Stage 3 (in my estimation) this is where the flow and making the connection are synonymous. If you take a look at the definition of the word *connection* you'll see that it is a linking of one thing to another or the link itself. The more you train the more you will be able to make more and more varied "links" in your actions. This is making the connection.

Counter The Counter

You strike. Your opponent defends and hits back. You defend against his hit back. That's simple enough, don't you think? Well, let's take a look of what that consists of.

First, you must know the angles of attack and styles of arnis. That's easy enough. Then you must know the different methods of defending against a strike, the different blockings and passings. Again, very easy.

Okay, now here's the kicker. You must know what you can do from your own position, especially from an extended strike (example: at the finish of #1 strike with your cane out there). You must know what your opponent can do from where he is at.

Explore the possibilities. Then you drill, drill, drill. One point I found out from my karate training is that an opponent usually will not set himself up to do an attack the hard way. He will usually go the easiest route of delivery. Nobody will make it intentionally tough on himself. This helps.

One can, from a brace defense against a #1 strike, counter with a #2 strike, a butt of the cane strike, an abaniko strike or slide down the cane and strike your hand with his cane. Did I leave anything out? Yes. Tons of possibilities.

You get the idea? It is one thing to reach out and hit your opponent. That is quite simple. Your attention/intention is on hitting them to a target or series of targets. To counter the counter you need to be able to *include your opponent.*

Most students are so centered on what they are going to do to their opponent that they are surprised by the counter attack. Their focus is so strong on hitting the opponent that they don't include the opponent in the equation. Then they react too late. This comes from *not* including the opponent in the fight. When you include your opponent, his actions will be an overall part of your actions.

As you can see, countering your partner's counter move is something which is a high degree of skill. It takes familiarization with a wide variety of Modern Arnis techniques so that you can recognize, at a split second's notice, what your partner is going to do and then to go ahead of him and reverse the situation. Prof. Presas was a master at this. Nearly every partner drill was some form of counter the counter development. This was conceptually finalized with the presentation of Tapi-Tapi.

Prof. Remy executing a cane lock on Brian Zawilinski

Cross Hand Training
Prof. Remy Presas was left handed. In the beginning, it must've been hard on him but it became his advantage later on. He was one of the best right handed stick fighters I have ever seen. And his left hand was better.

I remember a valuable lesson working with the Professor. We were doing a sparring drill and I disarmed him. I was quite embarrassed because I did not intend to do it. I went off of a reaction to an opening. I am also a believer in the Senior/Junior system and one does not try to embarrass your senior. He smiled and said to me, *"Danny. That was very good. But you forgot one thing. I am left handed. The cane was in my right hand."* He then switched hands and took me to school with the same drill, smiling all the while. He did not hurt me or get cross with me. I take it as he saw it was time for a new lesson, actually two lessons. The first was there are gradations of excellence. I had gotten to a point where he could "up the game" on me without my becoming introverted. The second lesson was to train the *cross hand.*

The Flow
I have saved the most important key aspect for last. The Flow needs to be experienced to be fully understood. Words don't quite do it but here goes. Workable basic definitions of the word flow are to come or go as in a stream and to proceed continuously and smoothly. The definitions are taken from the Random House dictionary.

You notice that a stream or river doesn't go along and then stop - and then start back up again and later on, stop - and start back up again when lunch is over, etc. It just goes along and keeps on going without halting around rocks and between land masses and sharp angles. It fits in and adapts and goes over, under, through obstacles without stopping motion.

That is the flow of a river and that is the Flow of Modern Arnis.

If you take a look at any hard style of martial art form you'll see stop and go actions. That is not the Flow. Arts like Japanese Aikido and Chinese Taiji have the Flow. Gymnastic high bar and uneven parallel bar exercises have the Flow. The gymnastic floor exercise will have a combination of the Flow with stops here and there. Figure skating is the Flow. A successful boxer is the Flow. Whether on offense or defense, there is this continual non-freeze action while doing something.

The reason I put the Flow at the last is so that after reading this far, you'll now have a frame of reference. If you can adapt, that is the Flow. If your timing is on, that is the Flow. When you do disarms, that is the Flow. If you have arm sensitivity you have the Flow. In terms of Modern Arnis, the Flow is the life in the art. I use this analogy because when you look at it, life is everywhere.

In Modern Arnis, the Flow is everywhere or else it isn't Modern Arnis.

Like I said, the Flow needs to be experienced and practiced. There is one good thing that I'd like to point out here. Like life, everybody has the Flow within themselves. It just needs to be nurtured.

The 6-count drill works the flow from an extended medium range.
The give and take drill works the flow in and out of medium range.
The cane sparring drills work the flow in close range. Flowing locks or pre-arranged drills in the arm sensitivity section are also good.

The first flow drill I learned is what I believe to be the mother of all flow drills, the basic flow drill. I demonstrate this very basic but very important drill on the next page.

Master that and the rest will integrate into your skill.

The basic flow drill of Modern Arnis.

#12 Strike - Highline banda y banda

#12 Strike - Highline banda y banda

#3 Strike - Mid-line banda y banda

#4 Strike - Mid-line banda y banda

Essays on Modern Arnis pt. 2 - Evolution

It is a well known fact that nothing entirely stays the same. Change occurs. Following Prof. Remy's journey, he began training with his grandfather, Leon. From there he expanded his training by connecting up with balintawak eskrima. He continued his research, including fighting a number of duels, and emigrated to the United States in 1975. His research didn't stop. He added Small Circle Jiu-Jitsu and some Ryukyu Kempo into his Modern Arnis applications. The point I'm making is that although he never changed the name of his art, Modern Arnis, the art kept evolving up to the point of his death.

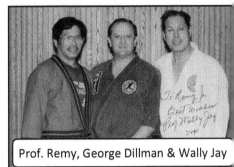

Prof. Remy, George Dillman & Wally Jay

Part two of this book details one of the branches that Modern Arnis took. This covers a bit of my journey.

Independence

How did my branch of Modern Arnis come about? In 1997 I faxed Prof. Remy a petition. I have the fax saved...somewhere. I'm not quite sure where I have it stashed but luckily for me, I did scan it for my memoirs. I was at a crossroads in my life. My daughter, Charlie, had just been born. She was child number six in my family with Marie but she was my first blood daughter, so to speak. I decided to come off of the seminar trail to raise my girl. The second crossroad was that I had a specifically designed Modern Arnis curriculum laid out for at least a decade by this time. I had said nothing to Prof. Remy about it but I felt now was time to ask permission for it to be recognized by him...or not. He was staying at the house of Bob Quinn when I sent him the fax. It read:

Dear Professor,   8 Aug 97

I would have liked to make it to both Michigan and Atlanta. I forgot when I talked to you in Portland that I had a seminar in L.A. at the same time as Michigan and the plans fell through for here. Sorry.

I have a formal request to make. I would like your permission to form my own branch of Modern Arnis, much like how Kajukenbo has different branches of it but is still under the main style of Kajukenbo. As you know, I have my own rank system and teaching system for my own school regarding Modern Arnis. It has proven very effective as you can see in my students Lynn, Tim and Tyler. I, personally, would feel better when teaching seminars and so forth, if I officially had my own branch of your art. I am working on publishing my second karate book and would like to do one on Modern Arnis as well as possibly a tape or two.

Two things to bear in mind:

1) This is not a Jeff Arnold/Mike Replogle thing where I am going to break off and start up an "American Freestyle Modern Arnis" sort of thing. You ARE my teacher, and Modern Arnis is YOUR creation. I just want to head my own branch of it.

2) I will abide by your decision if you feel that the time is not right or that I still need more training and understanding of your art or any other reason you have, you decide for me to not have my own branch, so be it. You'll have no complaint from me.

I am having Bob Quinn give this to you while I am not there so that you don't have me there waiting for an answer. That would drive a lot of people crazy.

Anyway, please call me at my home phone number when you have an answer. Also, I should be in Seattle when you do the seminar with Prof. Jay and Prof. Dillman.

All for now -
Dan Anderson

I met up with him at the Seattle seminar and softly broached the subject.

Me: *"Uhhhh, Professor. Did you get the fax I sent you?"*
Prof: *"Mmmmm, yes."*

Me: *"What do you think?"*
Prof: *"Mmmmm, yes."*

I took that as a sort of a yes but couldn't really say he said the words, "Yes, Dan. Form your own sub-system." I always wondered about it until Jimmy Thomas gave me a message from Bob Quinn in 2006. We were at the opening gala for The First Remy Presas Memorial Training Camp in Taygatay. I'd known Jimmy for a number of years. He came up to me and said, *"Mr. Quinn couldn't make it but he wanted me to deliver this to you."* He gave me the envelope which had this card in it.

Dan,
I had hoped to hand deliver this to you myself. I have entrusted my loyal student Jimmy Thomas to give you this. It has brought back many memories of when I sat down with the professor to read it and interoperate the contents. I remember how he would ask me "Bob what do you think?" My response of course was positive and well received by him. He said "this is a good thing" "Dan must do this".
Dan, I thank you for being a friend and on many occasions, an advisor.
I will speak with you when you get back.

Please look to see if some folks want to come to Atlanta for a camp.

My eyes teared up as I read this. This was the beginning to a great camp.

MA80 - Modern Arnis For The New Millennium

So, what is my branch of Modern Arnis all about? I have written quite a number of books on Modern Arnis and the MA80 System Arnis/Eskrima (my branch) but this is more of an essay book than a technical teaching manual so if you're interested in that aspect of what I do, you can check them out at the Super Dan Online Library.

David Fogge, senior student of the late Roland Dantes conducted two interviews with me where I went over Modern Arnis, the MA80 System and much more. I have edited and combined the interviews to set up sub-sections to create a better flow for reading.

The David Fogge Interview – Meeting Remy Presas

DF: *How long did you study Modern Arnis under Remy Presas?*
DA: I began training under Remy Presas in 1980 and have been active in Modern Arnis until his death in 2001. I received my 1st degree black belt in 1982 and my 6th degree black belt in 1994. I was awarded the title of Senior Master in 1995. I received permission to form my own sub-system in 1997.

How did you meet Professor Remy A. Presas and as a successful competition karate fighter, what was it which made you want to learn Modern Arnis from him?
I have told this story so often that I'm sure others can probably tell the tale better than I can now but for those who haven't heard it, I'll tell it again. This is an excerpt from my memoirs entitled, *Super Dan – A Martial Arts Memoir*:*

It was at the end of my career in national fighting when I was presented with an incredible opportunity. Mind you, if I had my way I would have blown the opportunity off in a heartbeat but it was the persistence of my next teacher that I didn't. The California State Karate Championships in 1980; it was at that tournament where I first met Remy Presas.

To set this up I have to back track a bit. Fred King was always bringing in this master or that master to his academy to teach seminars.

Each time he'd invite me to participate and I'd politely or impolitely refuse. Either way, I was not interested. I was a karate boy and not into tai chi, kung fu, chi development and whatever else he was presenting in the seminars. Well, Fred and I went to the CKC together. When I was there I found this "Professor guy" dogging our heels all the time. I couldn't get rid of him. I turn left there he was. I turn right there he was. I was afraid to look under the carpet. He was even staying in the room with us.

I remember waking up at 6:00 am to the sound of pat-pat-pat, pat-pat-pat. He and Fred were training already, practicing trapping hands. *"Guys. It's 6 in the morning! Come on!"* Silence. I wake up an hour later to hear the sound of clack-clack-clack, clack-clack-clack, off in the distance. They were doing double stick sinawali drills in the parking lot! Both of these guys are nuts!

During the intermission of the tournament, Fred and I and this "Professor guy" were up in our room and he was telling us about this time he was mugged in New York City. I still hadn't been able to shake this guy and this was irritating. He must've seen my eyes roll up in my head as he described how he got out of one assailant's grasp when he said, *"Dan, grab my wrist."* Aw geez, now I have to play audience participation? You've got to be kidding me.

The next moment altered the course of my martial arts career. I reluctantly grabbed his wrist. He executed a simple walk through wrist release that is seen in any standard jujutsu or aikido book, a very simple action. What struck me was his attitude. In the competitive ring I've seen all kinds of attitudes. I've seen everything from the incredible confidence of Jeff Smith to the blustering false bravado of (insert the name of whoever you don't like here). This was beyond anything I'd ever seen before. There was no consideration in his manner and execution that this action *wouldn't* work. He waltzed through it with the same difficulty as one would have taking a breath. Holy shit! And this is the guy I had been dissing for the better part of the weekend? I'm going to keep an eye on this guy. He had something I'd never seen before.

This was the beginning of a 21 year relationship. It didn't occur to me till much, much later that he was biding his time, waiting until I got off my high horse to recognize that he had something to offer. I'm glad he had the patience. Roughly 4-6 months later I took my first arnis seminar and I was struck by lightning for the second time in my life.

I still laugh at myself when I think of this. I'm glad he decided to suffer my big-headedness.

What was it about Professor Remy and Modern Arnis that appealed to you? What were the most impressive aspects of his art and of his skills?
Skill wise, I think the thing that appealed to me the most was that he had an answer for anything you threw at him. He was always one to three steps ahead of any of us and I found that intriguing. This was the stuff of legends I felt and this was a skill I wanted to attain. He was strong but he used his smoothness more than his strength. Just plain fascinating.

Coming from your karate and fighting background, what were your thoughts about Modern Arnis?
I found that Modern Arnis was the thing that I was looking for but I didn't know it yet. I was just a banger, a karate guy who was interested in kicking and punching. But there was one problem. I was getting less and less interested in competition karate, which was my bread and butter back then. What was I going to do when I finally dropped out of competition? I didn't know. And then Remy Presas appeared in my life. Modern Arnis contained workable weapons work, joint locking, throwing, flowing applications – everything that was missing from my karate training.

Was your previous training helpful or not?

Extremely helpful. I was already an analysis geek so I scrutinized every-thing the Professor did. I trained myself to be ambidextrous and that helped quite a bit. I wasn't trained in a stiff kind of karate so I was already fluid. The previous 14 years I spend in karate properly prepared me to learn arnis. I picked up the art as though I was born to it. I remem-ber Fred King telling me it looked as though I learned by osmosis. Not really but my extensive experience taught me how to watch someone and immediately discern their actions.

Has Modern Arnis affected/benefited your karate and vice versa? How?

Absolutely. The biggest effect of arnis on my martial arts is that my karate contains the Flow. I've described elsewhere that my concept of the Flow is 1. continuity of motion and, 2. recognition of option. All of my karate experience in the fighting arena is where it influences my arnis. I transpose my karate strategies and tactics to my sparring with a cane and it works beautifully.

The MA80 System Arnis/Eskrima

You now teach and practice a system called "MA80". How did this sys-tem come about?

The full title of it is the MA80 System Arnis/Eskrima. The first inkling of it came about when he went through a period of ill health back around 1987. I began to worry if he was going to die around then and wondered what I would do without him being around. It was then that I began re-searching the underlying principles that he was using (See the essay *Technical Pillars of Modern Arnis*). I stopped listening to him and began really watching him and feeling him when I was his demonstration dum-my. I paid great attention to him, especially when I was his *uke* (technique recipient). I learned a great deal this way. Fortunately he re-covered but I never stopped learning from him in this manner.

Originally, MA80 was a curriculum for my school regarding Modern Ar-nis. I didn't think of it as some-thing separate then. I asked Prof. Presas permission in 1997 to create a sub-system of my own. This was for the use in my school and it included a set progression with belt ranks and all that. He granted me that (See the essay *Independence*.). When he passed away I purposely called it Modern Arnis 80 or MA80 to set me apart from the natural hierarchy battle I foresaw coming. I neither needed nor wanted any part of that.

Did it naturally evolve from Modern Arnis or was it something you specifically set out to create?
It was a natural evolution. As I said it was a curriculum for the Modern Arnis I was teaching. Since Prof. Remy's death I continued to research Filipino martial arts in a more general way. I was fortunate enough to be introduced to Manong Ted Buot by Jaye Spiro. Manong Ted was a direct student of the founder of balintawak eskrima, Anciong Bacon. I began training with Manong Ted and this opened my eyes to another way of looking at things and this was the beginning of the MA80 evolution. I later worked out with Mark Wiley and his Integrated Eskrima system and again, my eyes were opened to yet another approach.

How would you define MA80?
The simple way of defining it is "Dan Arnis." I think the definition lies in the title and what it means. *MA* = two different things. The first is my base art *Modern Arnis.*

The second is what I personally do *Masid* (study or research of) Arnis. Quite often a student will see me doing something a bit different than what I am teaching them. That is *Masid Arnis.*

The *80* also has two meanings. The first is I began training with Prof. Remy in 19*80*. The second has to do with splitting the 8 and 0 apart. If you turn the number 8 on its side, you have an infinity symbol. When. Remy taught any given move, he would teach many different applications for it. This gave one the impression that there were infinite applications. I found out that when you surprised him, however, he was astonishingly direct. So, the 8-0 means *the possibility of anything* (8) *reduced to the simplicity of the moment* (0). That is the end goal of the MA80 System.

Since founding MA80, has it undergone an evolution or changes to the curriculum and physical aspects of the system from then to now? If so, so how?
MA80 began as my curriculum of what Prof. Remy's art. He didn't have any kind of proper curriculum in the United States anyway so I came up

with what made sense to me in my school and implemented that. I faxed him in 1997 and asked his permission to formulate my own sub-system and it was approved. That's how it started (See essay *Independence*).

Since then, my experience in balintawak eskrima and integrated eskrima plus all of the independent research I've involved myself in, the MA80 System Arnis/Eskrima has definitely evolved since its inception and continues to evolve to this day.

How much of MA80 is "Dan's" and how much is "Remy's"?
Hoo boy! What a loaded question! I suppose the first differentiation I would make is that MA80 is a Filipino/American art. The core art is Modern Arnis. That goes unquestioned. Remy Presas was my first and main teacher in Filipino martial arts. But at the same time I am an American who grew up in America. There are going to be cultural viewpoint differences. The second point I'd make is that the full title is MA80 System Arnis/Eskrima. This is to validate and acknowledge the influences of Manong Ted Buot and Mark Wiley, both Eskrimadors.

Since my teacher's death in 2001 I have moved on using modern arnis as the core of my understanding to carve my own path. I would guess that at this time, *technically*, MA80 is roughly 60% Remy's. I say technically because if you watched me move you could say, *"I remember Professor Presas doing that."* or some such. Mentally, however, the reverse ratio would be more the case. How I structure what I teach and more important, why I teach what I do and why I emphasize certain points over others are very much *"Dan-isms."*

Can you outline the areas of study covered in MA80?
The MA80 System Arnis/Eskrima is primarily single stick and empty hand based. That being said I include double stick and stick & dagger but not to the extent as single stick.

Does MA80 include blade work?
Yes. An expansion of what I was taught from Prof. Presas lies in more blade work. He didn't teach much blade work in the US. It was more stick oriented. I have added much more baston y daga (stick & dagger) as

well as espada y daga (sword & dagger) in the curriculum. I also include the modular knife program designed by another of the Professor's students, Bram Frank. MA80 contains applications of single stick, double stick, stick & dagger, bolo & dagger weapons work as well as empty handed striking, locking, and throwing arts. It is very well rounded.

Do you believe there are specific areas of MA80 which are more important than other parts or are all aspects just as important?
For me, single stick and empty hand applications are the most important.

Is MA80 an "officially recognized" style? And if so, who has recognized it?
Yes. The first to recognize it was Prof. Presas himself when he gave me permission to form my own sub-system. After his death I petitioned several of his peers including Prof. Wally Jay and Dr. Maung Gyi for recognition of MA80 as a separate style. I had not been introduced to any of the Modern Arnis practitioners in the Philippines at that time.

The summer of 2006 I traveled to the Philippines along with Bram Frank and Brian Zawilinski to teach in the 1st Remy Presas Memorial Training Camp and the 3rd World Filipino Martial Arts Festival. I met the most senior student of Prof. Presas, Cristino Vasquez, Rodel Dagooc, Rene Tongson and a number of the older brothers. It was a great experience. It was there I became one of the founding members of the Worldwide Family of Modern Arnis and MA80 was recognized as one of the founding groups. I have since received a certificate from the senior masters as well recognizing MA80 as a valid and separate branch of Modern Arnis. I recently received a letter of support from one of Prof. Presas' closest friends and senior master in Modern Arnis as well, Roland Dantes. My most recent recognition was the promotion of Lakan Sampu, 10th Dan by Grand Master Roberto Presas (upcoming section). All of this means a great deal to me because it validates the fact that I am on the right track.

Although all styles were created by someone at some point, it is neverthe-less often viewed as controversial to create a new style. What would you say to those who question if you should be creating a style?
If we were sitting over coffee discussing the matter, then I would point out a number of facts.

First of all, this is exactly the same thing Remy, himself, did. He trained in the family system. He left home and found and trained in balintawak eskrima. He left there and went back home and continued his research until he came up with the art of Remy Presas, which he named Modern Arnis. This is actually the evolution of any style of any kind of martial art. The student learns, figures it out from a number of sources, finds out what works for him and what appeals to him, does his own thing, end of story. The list of names goes on and on – Remy Presas, Ed Parker, Bruce Lee, Chuck Norris, Jigoro Kano, et al.

Second, I liken how Prof. Presas taught Modern Arnis to how Donghaichuan taught baguazhang. Dong had different students who had previously trained in other martial arts. He taught each student according to his past training. They all learned the same principles but you now see baguazhang schools with different emphasis points. Yin Fu did northern Shaolin so you see a lot of quick light movement in the Yin school. Chengtinghua was a wrestler so you see more throwing applications in the Cheng school of bagua. Which one is right? They both are. The same is with any of the branches of modern arnis today.

Third, I did the same back in 1977 when I founded American Freestyle Karate and that is still going strong so time will tell with MA80, won't it.

Are you still researching, analysing and evolving MA80 and if so, which areas?
My current study is in the area of traditional arnis or classical arnis and how it fits in with the latter developments of Prof. Remy. We were taught those but they fell by the wayside in the very early 1990s. Seeing that they are more distance based, I feel they have a place in my own expression of the art.

When teaching, do you teach MA80 arnis and karate separately or is there a natural blending of the two?
I teach them separately as they are two entirely different curriculums.

Aside from Remy Presas' teaching and your own innovations, who or what else has had an influence on MA80?
Let me go over a list of names who I consider are the "Pillars of MA80."

Remy Presas. That one is obvious. He was my teacher for 21 years.

Manong Ted Buot had a tremendous influence on me (He passed away in 2013). It's funny because I have had the least amount of lessons from him of all his students. He lived in an outskirt of Detroit so I had not the chance to really train with him much but what I've had has been electric and very down to earth. To be truthful, any FMA right now has some sort of impact on me. I love seeing the variations or movement and where they connect with what I have been taught. I remember thinking how fortunate I was to have trained under Prof. Remy when I went to the first

FMA gathering in Oakland, Cali-  fornia. I saw many different styles of arnis and Eskrima performed beautifully but I was not *surprised* by what I saw. I had seen it already from Prof. Presas. There are aspects of drills that I have taken from different systems as well to augment what I do.

Mark Wiley (Integrated Eskrima) is another influence that I'd like to acknowledge. We got in communication and we were brothers right from the start. We think alike although we have totally different FMA upbringings. When I got together with him in Philadelphia we sparred a bit. He exposed some holes in my defense and operating method and then showed me how to close them. It was like I was back on the competition circuit again. It was great.

Punong Guro Edgar Sulite. Punong Guro Edgar did the same thing with eskrima that I did with karate. He trained with many masters, travelled the Philippines and came up with his own system, called Lameco Eskrima. He was, in my eyes, the "Super Dan of the Philippines."

Grand Master Bobby Taboada. I got from him how he generates power in his striking. GM Bobby was a boxer and uses body torque much like a boxer when he strikes. I am initially a karate trained fighter and I use my hips to generate power.

Antonio "Tatang" Ilustrisimo. I have only seen videos of "Tatang" move but they always remind me to keep it simple and to be able to move from any position.

Punong Guro Edgar Sulite   Antonio Ilustrisimo and Mark Wiley

Has your karate had any influence on the formation of MA80?
Absolutely! It was the fact that I was a well versed karate fighter that I think really helped me. As an open style national champion I found it was in my best interests to be as well rounded as possible. Karate-wise, I trained in many different techniques and approaches as I could. I used this viewpoint in my arnis training.

I am also very analytical in my approach. I study and study to find out what makes things work. I worked on being as ambidextrous as possible and to be as versed in all aspects of arnis that Prof. Presas taught. I was also taught in karate to think of, first and foremost, to be effective. I kept this in the forefront of my approach to Modern Arnis as Prof. Presas was a fighter. Anybody who knows his history knows he was quite a fighter in his formative days and that his techniques were "road tested."

When I trained I kept this in mind. This is where he and I related best, I feel. He saw me as a fighter and taught me as such. My karate sparring has influenced my stick sparring/fighting tremendously as well. In the early days of karate competition, your strike had to have enough power and focus to disable your opponent if you decided to land it with full force. I use this concept when stick sparring. As a stick is an impact weapon, it is used to break things with that impact. My targets are hard, bony areas that will not withstand such an impact. I go for something that will end the fight on the first or second shot. This comes from my karate training. My concepts of distancing, timing, targeting and so on are all karate fighting concepts that I use.

Did you observe any changes in his teaching or methods during that time? If so, what did you think of these changes?
Yes. Initially the change was from a larger, more circular locking format to a tighter, sharper application. It was his work with Prof. Wally Jay of the Small Circle Jiu-Jitsu system that brought about this change. What did I think? It was more painful! That's what I thought. I marveled at it because Prof. Remy was great at locking to begin with and now he got better. Ow! He also introduced some of the dumog (Filipino wrestling) in the 1990s but I was not so much interested in this aspect. I loved his locking, body management skills and stick work the best.

What would you say are the key differences between the Modern Arnis you were taught and the MA80 you now teach and practice?
Most Modern Arnis in the USA was taught at seminars. It was very broad shoot and the curriculum was non-existent. The best way I can describe it was he threw a fist full of confetti up in the air and when it came down; whatever stuck to you was what you came away with. That used to drive many of us around the bend. A number of the senior students would come to him with a curriculum or belt ranking schematic but none of them ever were used.

MA80 is very structured in a linear fashion, very progression oriented. What is meant by a linear fashion is that each level of progression is a set up basis for the next level. I compare it to how the American school system is supposed to be set up. You don't go on to the second grade until you have graduated from the first grade and so on. My goal for any student is at least 1st degree black belt so everything prior to that is basically laying the foundation. This requires lots of practice on basics and the drills which will produce this product.

Another key difference is that I stress alignment, structure and leveraging far more than Prof. Remy did. When I began karate I was a skinny 14 year old kid. There was no such thing as a Juniors Class. I was in with the adults right off the bat. I was the little guy. I had to think things through and utilize what I had in the most efficient manner. This meant learning, understanding and using principles rather than relying on physical attributes alone. This took me a long time to figure out. Even though now I'm an adult I still think like a little guy. I am also 56 years older than when I began martial arts and the body is not as fast and supple as it once was. I now need to rely on principles and their applications even more than ever. So, this is what I stress for every student right from the beginning.

What innovations have you made that are different from Professor's orig-inal teachings as far as technique is concerned?
The key innovations regarding Prof. Presas' Modern Arnis that I have made are in the technical explanations of what he taught. If you didn't know what he was doing or couldn't follow what he was doing, he was "magical." He was tremendously skilled and his applications often felt like magic but there is one thing for sure and that he was human. He was a "white belt" at the beginning of his training, too. It is so easy to overlook that aspect. Every master was a beginner. Every master made the same stupid beginners mistakes we all made. The key thing is that they overcame whatever obstacles they faced and eventually mastered their art. They did it and so can we. How did they do it? They, by whatever means they accomplished it, ended up having a complete understanding of their art.

My first inroads to Modern Arnis were when I began to understand what Remy Presas was doing on a principle level. That opened the door for me. Technically I have created a number of drills that all lead to the two key pillars of Modern Arnis which are *the flow* and *counter the counter*. Now, that's regarding my teacher's art.

What are the techniques and strategies of MA80?
The fighting strategies of the MA80 System align with and stem from the offensive and defensive fighting approaches outlined in my first book, *American Freestyle Karate: A Guide To Sparring*.* The offensive approaches for stick fighting are:
1. Direct attack (single shot)
2. Attack by combination (two or more attacks, each intending to hit)
3. Indirect attack (fakes, feints and attention getters prior to the real attack)

The defensive approaches I use are:
1. Hit as the ranges cross/instant counter (you step forward and strike as your opponent moves forward)
2. Defang (immediate strike to your opponent's weapon wielding hand)
3. Block and hit or pass and hit (you defend stick against stick and then hit back)
4. Evade and hit (step back out of the way and return with a counter strike).

What are fighting principles of MA80?
The principles of MA80 are the same as in my curriculum of karate. They are:
1. Monitoring (attack recognition)
2. Timing (a decision of when)
3. Structure (maintaining personal body alignment)
4. Alignment (maximizing one's alignment with your partner/opponent)
5. Zanshin (perfect finish, keeping the first four in play when you have finished your action) and
6. Flow.

www.superdanonlinelibrary.com

Are you still researching, analysing and evolving MA80 and if so, which areas?

My current study is in the area of traditional arnis or classical arnis and how it fits in with the latter developments of Prof. Remy. We were taught those but they fell by the wayside in the very early 1990s. Seeing that they are more distance based, I feel they have a place in my own expression of the art.

When teaching, do you teach MA80 arnis and karate separately or is there a natural blending of the two?

I teach them separately as they are two entirely different curriculums.

Do you intend to create and maintain a ranking hierarchy within MA80 to avoid some of the issues associated with Modern Arnis in the past?

Yes. One of the reasons there are so many different groups of modern arnis currently is because Prof. Presas never truly established a pecking order that *he enforced*. The key words are *he enforced*. There are a number of legitimate senior students of his (myself included) who are all forwarding the art in our own manners.

We are something like Shotokan karate. Shotokan had one founder, Gichin Funakoshi, but has many, many variations. As MA80 is its own separate entity, there is a definite pecking order to short circuit any divisiveness that could come about. MA80, however, is not big enough for that to be a real concern at this time.

With your extensive background in sport karate, what are the chances of increasing the visibility of MA80 within the tournament circuit, including empty hands as well as weapons, or is this even an issue?

I keep MA80 apart from sport karate and sport arnis. It is more art and self-defense oriented.

What are the primary differences in teaching philosophy between the way we learned from the Professor in the 80's and the way you are teaching students new to Arnis/Eskrima today?

Many of us first heard of Modern Arnis with the term *The Art Within Your Art*. This was Prof. Remy's way of introducing Modern Arnis to a wide number of martial artists from many disciplines. Remember during the late 1970's, seminars were mostly in-house. A kenpo man didn't go to a taekwondo man's seminar and so forth. A genius of Prof. Remy's was to find the common threads between the different martial arts and show how Modern Arnis had commonality with all of them while maintaining the Filipino martial art. He made Modern Arnis accessible to everyone.

A key point to make at this juncture is that even though Prof. Remy marketed his seminars as *The Art Within Your Art*, he didn't water down what he taught. The difference between his marketing concept and the art he taught is important to understand as there have been others, including senior students who have made this mistake of thinking that *The Art Within Your Art* approach was watered down Modern Arnis. It wasn't.

Filipino martial arts are so much more widespread now, so when I teach at seminars I am teaching, for the most part, people who have already had some FMA experience. Where they do not have that experience I begin by teaching them some of a program I developed called the Fast Track Arnis Training Program. This program is based on a very simple template of motion from which all the strikes, blocks, disarms and so forth are based upon. It is a very successful approach.

Do you see MA80 progressing as a stand-alone art in itself or as "the art within your art" as the Professor promoted it?

Don't be fooled by his *The Art Within Your Art* marketing slogan. Modern Arnis was *always* taught as a stand-alone art. MA80 has also *always* been a stand-alone art. None of it has ever relied on my karate teaching. I have developed a couple of sub-programs within the MA80 System which are stand-alone as well. MA80 is its own entity.

What makes MA80 unique and different to other martial arts?
I hope this doesn't come across as a snide of flip answer but what makes MA80 different or unique is that it is the *Super Dan approach*. I like to feel that there is something in the Super Dan approach that anyone from any system can use to make their own expression better. There is a ton of background karate experience that I can draw on from my career as one of the top fighters in the nation. Back in my karate competition days, I was known as a crafty and analytical fighter. I also research like crazy so that I can continue to increase my understanding. When you understand something, you can utilize it to your advantage and not be the adverse effect of it. All of this is layered into the MA80 System.

In teaching Modern Arnis/MA80, how are you similar to Professor and in what ways different?
There is not much in the way of similarities except for one thing. I am far more nurturing as a teacher now than I was twenty years ago. I am more inspirational to my students. How I am different is that I am a technical and principle geek. For the beginner, there is a right way and wrong way to execute and I am very strict on that. Lay a proper foundation right from the start.

What are your plans for the future especially with MA80? What direction do you see it going in? Is it continuing evolving?
I do not kid myself in thinking I am laying the groundwork for a system that will survive me. America is not like that. The American and western cultures are not one of time and tradition. I do not see any one student who will become the successor to what I am doing now. It sort of sucks but those are the hard and cold facts of the part of the world I live in.

MA80 will live on through my works until other works become more interesting to practitioners. Is MA80 continuing to evolve? Absolutely. I was telling Roger Agbulos (student of the late Edgar Sulite) that *"the house is not fully built yet."* I am not done with my explorations. It is far from completed. I am learning all the time. I see new innovations or refine what I do to make applications more effective. It is far from being a done deal. MA80 will be done when I am done and not a moment before.

Regarding Modern Arnis & Remy Presas

As the seniors of Professor Remy pass and there are less of them, how do you see Modern Arnis being taught and changing?

I don't know how much change is occurring as I don't have much contact with the seniors in the Philippines. I do know that Samuel "Bambit" Dulay (right) has been running a bit of parallel course as I am in that he has lately been emphasizing the classical or traditional methods of Modern Arnis as well as the more recent (circa 1997) Tapi-Tapi development. Each of the seniors in the US have been doing the same, creating curriculums based on what they got from Prof. Remy influenced by their own personal and martial backgrounds.

This is a fascinating point in its evolution. Since Modern Arnis was *never* strictly "this way or that way," it is very malleable, very flexible. You examine the teachings of me, Kelly Worden, Dieter Knuttel, Roland Rivera, Bruce Chiu, Bram Frank, Brian Zawilinski, Chad Bailey, Doug Pierre, Tom Bolden, Chuck Gauss, Ken Smith, Gaby Roloff...the list goes on and on. You'll see differences and similarities in each of their methods of presentation and instruction. The common thread is that we all learned from Remy Presas.

Professor Remy taught and promoted Modern Arnis and FMA continuously for decades. Do you feel his contributions to FMA worldwide have been overlooked?

I don't think so much overlooked but in this day and age of rapid change, he is being slowly forgotten. It's been over 20 years since he passed away. Unless you're Elvis or Bruce Lee, no one stays in the limelight that long after you die. So, as long as the senior students keep his name alive he will be remembered but someday he will be like Gichin Funakoshi, more of as a historical figure.

Professor Presas concentrated on promoting Modern Arnis and the art instead of how the he taught in the Philippines. Do you think it was a smart approach?

It was smart and not so smart. It was smart in that he broke through to other martial artists and showed how Modern Arnis could fit within their base arts. That was brilliant. The only problem was that he didn't have any kind of set curriculum nor did he have exacting standards as to how the techniques were to be performed. That set up Modern Arnis to be looked upon as a weaker art in terms of fighting amongst other arnisadors or Eskrimadors. That was not so good.

Dan, having seen footage of you teaching, you are a skilled communicator and have excellent teaching skills/ability. In your opinion, how was Professor Remy as a teacher and through the years did you see his teaching skills and methodologies evolve?

Thank you. As a technical instructor, he wasn't scientific. As a practitioner he was terrific. So, it was up to students like me, Kelly Worden, Bram Frank, Brian Zawilinski, Dieter Knuttel, etc. to collect and coordinate the techniques, discern the principles and figure out how to teach them and all will be set. Did his methodologies evolve? I don't really think so. What he taught evolved but *how* he taught didn't, in my opinion.

As an innovator and empowerer, he was second to none, in my opinion. He inspired thousands to train in FMA. He was the epitome of an inspirational instructor. He was truly yin/yang.

With the passing of Professor Remy, there was, as expected, a period of political turmoil in the Modern Arnis world for a while. Thankfully it seems the seniors of the system have put aside politics to focus on passing on the art for the betterment/advancement of the system. Would you agree?

To a degree. I think what has occurred more so is that each Modern Arnis group is no longer engaged in having upsets with each other. That being said, there are certain individuals who I gravitate more towards because of shared martial values and personal compatibilities. There are a couple whom I will have nothing to do with because of lack of shared martial values and personal incompatibilities. Such is life.

When Prof. Remy died, he left no heir, so to speak. In most martial arts systems or groups which have one leader, when the leader dies the torch is passed to whoever is next in line. Well, that didn't happen. One of Prof. Presas' quirks was he would make whoever he was around feel like they were the golden boy or golden girl of the system. Outside of the numerical grades, there really wasn't any kind of hierarchy. The king had no number one son or daughter who was going to be crowned next.

So, Prof. Remy dies and there's a lot of squabbles of "who's on first." Who is really the top ranked or the highest student because *"Remy said..."*? It was a mess. A lot like American Kenpo Karate when Ed Parker died. As Tommy Lee Jones said in his first line in the movie, *The Fugitive*: *"My, my, my, my, my. What a mess!"* In the long run, a number of the top students formed their own groups and went about the business of running them. Each of us has one main common ground upon which to agree on: Modern Arnis is our base art and it was founded by Remy Presas. From there we go our own way.

The senior students of Professor Remy each taught their own interpretations of what they learnt from him with similar yet unique flavour and the art allowed for the individual to grow in their own way. Would you agree?

Absolutely. As we are all different human beings with different backgrounds and mindsets, it is natural to have our own flavor of the art. An example is that I haven't lived the life of Kelly Worden or Brian Zawilinski so my expression won't be the same as theirs. Kelly was a street kid while Brian worked as a corrections officer for 27 years. It works the same in reverse. Neither of them were even remotely close to being a hotshot karate champion like I was. We all have different backgrounds and life experiences so we will all have different flavors of the art despite having the same teacher. This is human nature.

Logically there are positives and negatives for Modern Arnis or any martial arts system evolving and being altered. What in your opinion are they?
The positives are figuring out a more efficient way of performing techniques. The negatives are changing something in order to be different than someone else or because the move looks more cool this way. The further you step away from application, the cooler something tends to look. Skilled and efficient application tends to look really basic and boring.

The culture of any country and the laws of the land will alter what and how any martial art is taught as well. The USA, for example, is a culture which does not condone violence. If you use martial arts to defend yourself and wind up in a court of law having to defend why you used it, you are going to have a rough go of it. Now take that a step further. If you used a blade or impact weapon, you're pretty much toast. So naturally, the methods of teaching and execution are going to alter because of the potential legalities involved.

Here is a reprint of an article that I included in my book *The North American Legacy of Remy Presas* that really says it all.* While it does not claim to be the law for all 50 states, it gives a sobering overview of what is involved in the legal viewpoint of self-defense. It's a lot more involved than just fighting back.

What Is Self-Defense?
Self-defense is defined as the right to prevent suffering force or violence through the use of a sufficient level of counteracting force or violence. This definition is simple enough on its face, but it raises many questions when applied to actual situations. For instance, what is a sufficient level of force or violence when defending oneself?

https://www.findlaw.com/criminal/criminal-law-basics/self-defense-overview.html

114

What goes beyond that level? What if the intended victim provoked the attack? Do victims have to retreat from the violence if possible? What happens when victims reasonably perceive a threat even if the threat doesn't actually exist? What about when the victim's apprehension is subjectively genuine, but objectively unreasonable? As you can see, self-defense law is more complicated than it first appears. In order to handle the myriad situations where self-defense arises, states have developed rules to determine when self-defense is allowed and how much force a victim can use to protect themselves. As mentioned, the exact rules differ between states, but the considerations are largely the same.

Is the Threat Imminent?
As a general rule, self-defense only justifies the use of force when it is used in response to an immediate threat. The threat can be verbal, as long as it puts the intended victim in an immediate fear of physical harm. Offensive words without an accompanying threat of immediate physical harm, however, do not justify the use of force in self-defense. Moreover, the use of force in self-defense generally loses justification once the threat has ended. For example, if an aggressor assaults a victim but then ends the assault and indicates that there is no longer any threat of violence, then the threat of danger has ended. Any use of force by the victim against the assailant at that point would be considered retaliatory and not self-defense.

Was the Fear of Harm Reasonable?
Sometimes self-defense is justified even if the perceived aggressor didn't actually mean the perceived victim any harm. What matters in these situations is whether a "reasonable person" in the same situation would have perceived an immediate threat of physical harm. The concept of the "reasonable person" is a legal conceit that is subject to differing interpretations in practice, but it is the legal system's best tool to determine whether a person's perception of imminent danger justified the use of protective force. To illustrate, picture two strangers walking past each other in a city park. Unbeknownst to one, there is a bee buzzing around his head. The other person sees this and, trying to be friendly, reaches quickly towards the other to try and swat the bee away. The person with the bee by his head sees a

stranger's hand dart towards his face and violently hits the other person's hand away. While this would normally amount to an assault, a court could easily find that the sudden movement of a stranger's hand towards a person's face would cause a reasonable man to conclude that he was in danger of immediate physical harm, which would render the use of force a justifiable exercise of the right of self-defense. All this in spite of the fact that the perceived assailant meant no harm; in fact, he was actually trying to help!

Imperfect Self-defense
Sometimes a person may have a genuine fear of imminent physical harm that is objectively unreasonable. If the person uses force to defend themselves from the perceived threat, the situation is known as "imperfect self-defense." Imperfect self-defense does not excuse a person from the crime of using violence, but it can lessen the charges and penalties involved. Not every state recognizes imperfect self-defense, however. For example, a person is waiting for a friend at a coffee shop. When the friend arrives, he walks toward the other person with his hand held out for a handshake. The person who had been waiting genuinely fears that his friend means to attack him, even though this fear is totally unreasonable. In order to avoid the perceived threat, the person punches his friend in the face. While the person's claim of self-defense will not get him out of any criminal charges because of the unreasonable nature of his perception, it could reduce the severity of the charges or the eventual punishment. Some states also consider instances where the person claiming self-defense provoked the attack as imperfect self-defense. For example, if a person creates a conflict that becomes violent then unintentionally kills the other party while defending himself, a claim of self-defense might reduce the charges or punishment, but would not excuse the killing entirely.

Proportional Response
Self-defense law requires the response to match the level of the threat in question. In other words, a person can only employ as much force as required to remove the threat. If the threat involves deadly force, the person defending themselves can use deadly force to counteract the threat. If, however, the threat involves only minor force and the

person claiming self-defense uses force that could cause grievous bodily harm or death, the claim of self-defense will fail.

Duty to Retreat

The original laws regarding self-defense required people claiming self-defense to first make an attempt to avoid the violence before using force. This is also known as a "duty to retreat." While most states have removed this rule for instances involving the use of nonlethal force, many states still require that a person make an attempt to escape the situation before applying lethal force.

Stand Your Ground

In contrast to the duty to retreat, many states have enacted so-called "stand your ground" laws. These laws remove the duty to retreat and allow for a claim of self-defense even if the claimant did nothing to flee from the threat of violence. As mentioned above, this is the more common rule when situations involve nonlethal force. State self-defense laws are split on the stand your ground principle when lethal force is in play, however.

Castle Doctrine

Even in states that require a person to retreat from the threat of imminent harm before defending themselves, a person can often use deadly force against someone who unlawfully enters their home. This rule, also known as "the castle doctrine," allows people to defend their homes against intruder through lethal force. Like most of these rules, the exact result will vary according to the jurisdiction and the specific facts of the case, so it's always a good idea to consult an attorney to learn more.

Well, that's pretty sobering. How does this play into "martial arts systems and evolving"? As stated above, the evolution of martial arts takes into consideration the culture and legalities of that culture. Let's look at the evolution of Filipino martial arts. Up through World War II FMA was a combat art. Jose Y Banco Presas taught the Filipino guerrillas to fight in the jungle. Leo Giron (Bahala Na system) was a guerilla fighter. Antonio Ilustrisimo and Anciong Bacon have certified kills under their belts. Combat arts.

After World War II, FMA morphed primarily into a dueling art. There were so-called "death matches" but in general they were more like duels. A fighter had a second, the match was held publicly or privately, the fight ended at first injury or when the second called it over and so forth. It was still "roughneck and thug" business but it wasn't kill-or-be-killed combat. This is the type of thing Prof. Remy participated in. Prof. Remy shifted his emphasis from dueling and fighting over to self-defense and physical culture. I don't know how the laws in the Philippines are but this fits in perfectly with the laws of the United States. There is a lot of internet talk about how the martial arts have been watered down and so on. In my opinion, martial arts have been put into a legal strangle hold as far as application possibilities go.

This sets the stage for "modernization" in terms of expanded training drills, extra moves and the like. Combat is simple or else you get hurt. Okay, rant over.

Professor Remy helped reignite interest in FMA in the Philippines and due to threats to his life, he had no choice but to leave the Philippines and travel to the USA. Did he reminisce or discuss his life in the Philippines?
He would speak of it now and again but he never went into great detail. Not with me at least. Much later on I found out a lot of his early years from two specific interviews. One was a videoed interview conducted by Joe Rebelo and the other was an audio interview conducted by Gaby Roloff and provided to me by Dieter Knuttel. Transcriptions of these interviews are the basis for the historical section of my book, *Modern Arnis – The Martial Art of Remy Presas.**

In the USA, would it be fair to say Professor Remy's focus changed to being more about promoting Modern Arnis and FMA in ways which would be accepted better by Americans?
Absolutely. First of all he had to break through a very insular group of American martial artists. Prior to his series of seminars, stylists tended to stick to their own. That is to say, it would be rare for a taekwondo player to go to a karate seminar and so forth. Prof. Remy changed all that with his slogan *The Art Within Your Art*. He presented arnis in such a way that

*www.superdanonlinelibrary.com

it blended with people's base arts.

The second thing is that he was driven with the idea of promoting Filipino culture. He stated that over and over again. He was not really concerned with developing good fighters per se. Now let's add to that the fact that most American martial artists are more hobby driven than they are fighting driven so most of the people training in Modern Arnis wanted the "sizzle" and not so much the "steak."

Though Modern Arnis encompasses Largo, Medio and Corto ranges. Would you say Modern Arnis focuses primarily on medium and close range?
Remy Presas Modern Arnis is definitely medium and close range based. I try to maintain a balance between all three ranges. What I found out in my karate career was that any area you were deficient in was going to come back and bite you in the end. If a guy was a good kicker, you jammed his kicks and punched him. If he was a great puncher, you stayed away and kicked him. This was a basic tenet of how I applied myself in karate free-fighting. Become skilled at all ranges. If you look at my first book, you'll notice that I add in-fighting techniques and clinch techniques. While they are common today, they weren't common at all back in 1980. I apply the same attitude to the MA80 System.

Regarding Balintawak Eskrima Influence

Was Professor Remy having learnt Balintawak a factor in you learning Balintawak from Teddy Buot?

Absolutely. I remember doing an exercise with Rich Parsons and later doing a demonstration with Jaye Spiro and they shared something in common. There was a "stickiness" to what their check hand was doing that was impeding my flow of motion. I remember Jaye telling me of an instructor in Detroit that taught balintawak eskrima. This was after Prof. Remy had died so I was rudderless at the time. Jaye was very impressed by Manong Ted and at my request, arranged for us to meet. Our meeting is really a funny story.

Manong Ted taught "old school" – one on one in private lesson style. I tagged along with Jaye for one of her lessons to watch. The lesson got underway and not before long, Manong Ted asked me what I would do against a move they were working on. I got up and began to show him and he immediately countered me. It wasn't speed or strength. It was timing and precision. He did this two more times during Jaye's lesson. The third time he did this I burst out laughing. He shut me down effortlessly. Well, you get shut down that easily by someone that skilled, there are only two things you can do about it – get pissed off or enjoy the hell out of it. I luxuriated in it. Here was a 71 year old man shutting me down with little apparent effort. Yeehah!

I find now that I am approaching my 70th birthday (November 2022), that last line is very funny. At the time I considered Manong Ted as being old. At this point he was only one year older than I will be in a couple months of this writing. What is even funnier is that when I first trained with Remy Presas, I was amazed at how well he moved for being so *old*! He was 45 at the time! Perspectives…

Back to meeting Manong Ted. At the end of Jaye's lesson he asked me why I wanted to learn balintawak. I told him that balintawak was one of the base arts of Modern Arnis and I wanted to learn it so that I could understand my teacher better. I was accepted as his student. Due to the fact that he lived in Detroit and I was in Oregon, we met rarely and I only had a handful of lessons from him prior to his stroke.

Did training in Balintawak and seeing where Professor Remy was coming from originally answer any questions, etc. you had from your Modern Arnis training?

Yes. There was spontaneity to his actions when you surprised him. He was astonishingly direct when he wanted to be. I believe this was a result of his balintawak training. The same with his use of the check hand. After training in balintawak under Manong Ted, I really see the connection there as well.

How did Balintawak affect your Modern Arnis? Do the systems complement each other?

What little balintawak I did changed my arnis tremendously. Manong Ted was a totally different teacher than Prof. Remy. He was precision and timing based. I remember my first lesson. The opening 45 minutes was going over how to generate power in the strike. 45 minutes! My legs were fried after that. He stressed economy of motion, the *preferred* or *optimum* action as well as really integrating the check hand in what you do. It really changed my arnis for the better I believe. I think the systems do complement each other although balintawak is more dueling based while Modern Arnis is more martial *art* based.

At close range, modern arnis and Balintawak are effective when applied correctly. What do you feel are its strengths at this range, why and what can ensure its effectiveness?

The use of the check hand is the key. Manong Ted called the check hand the *quarterback*. Guro Dan Inosanto said the check hand was more important than the cane hand. If you use the check hand to immobilize, to delay, to manage your opponent's cane or his check hand, you can dominate. As a last resort you can also punch him with your empty hand. In the words of Prof. Remy, *"There are so many things you can do."*

Ted Buot and Remy Presas

General Questions

You were the only non-Filipino awarded the title of Senior Master. How did that make you feel at the time and thinking back?

At the time I didn't give it a whole lot of thought. I was never a numbers or titles chaser so I filed it away in the back of my mind and left it there until I was researching for writing an encyclopedia of Modern Arnis. It was then when I found out that the only other Senior Masters in Modern Arnis were from the homeland. Since there were three more types of titles in the US (Punong Guro, Datu and Master of Tapi-Tapi), I wasn't sure where it fit in the overall whole. And to be honest, there was already too much muscle flexing over whose title superseded who's after Prof. Remy died, I didn't want to really get into it. I recently did get curious about it so I contacted one of the Senior Masters in the Philippines, Rene Tongson, to get some insight into it. Here is the conversation.

Me: *Here is a question for you. You, Cristino, Jerry and a couple of others in the PI were given the title Senior Master. I was the only person outside of the PI that Remy gave the title to. He never said anything about what it meant within the Modern Arnis structure. Can you give me any insight to this?*

Rene: The time gap between Lakan 5 to a GM Lakan 8 will require a transition. With the curriculum plus dedication the system has developed a good number of good practitioners who reached the Level considered in Modern Arnis as Masters. As they dedicate farther, a number of new Masters Level would again come. The older or those who were ahead had to get a separate distinction. They are seniors. Senior Masters.

Me: *I received Lakan 6 (6ᵗʰ Dan) on the same day.*
Rene: Remy gave you the distinction as the more senior of Masters on the same day.

Looking at it in this light, I feel honored.

Your books on Modern Arnis, MA80 and Arnis are of excellent quality with heaps of information. How many books have you written now and with your FMA books in particular, what are your goals?

Thank you. I've written around 20 books on arnis and have produced at least 50-60 DVDs on the subject as well. My overriding goal is this – to make it easier for the student to understand and take their game to the next level. I believe anyone can aspire to and attain grandmaster skills. They need dedication, of course, but what will really help them is an understanding of what they are doing both technically and using principles. This is and always has been my goal with my writings and video production.

What are the essential basics of MA80 and how do you ensure students appreciate their importance and develop them to a high standard?

On a broad note regarding the essential basics of MA80, structure, alignment, leveraging and positioning are the foundations of what I teach. I am not a big guy so I cannot rely on brute force to accomplish my aims. I rely on the above for my foundational skills.

From there I work to develop the Flow. As I said before, my concept of the Flow is the combination of continuity of motion and recognition of option. This means if I train in a wide number of techniques and become skilled at them, I will have a larger tool box. I will be able to recognize what will need to come out of the tool box at the appropriate moment. In my view of thinking, recognition is senior to analytical thought. Recognition is not reaction. Reaction is blind action. Recognition turns into appropriate counter action.

Once students develop a strong foundation and base and understanding through quality training and instruction, is there a freedom within the system and its techniques?

Yes and no. In America, freedom of expression usually turns out to being the student wanting to do their own thing before becoming really skilled. They get several good techniques under their belts and want to specialize in those. This is a trap because if you can counter the counter, they will become victims of their own impatience. I've done this so many times with others.

Two examples to illustrate this come to mind. In 2005 I was staying a week with Dee Childress (right). Dee trained under the late Bob Quinn and was a co-promoter of a Modern Arnis camp we had done together. He was huge on applying the finishing move. I was working with him on the concept of counter the counter but he would always want to apply the finishing move right away. So, I exchanged a rattan stick for a padded one. Every time he would try to apply a finishing move on me, I countered it and tapped him with the padded stick saying *"You don't want to*  *do that."* It took a number of repetitions to get him to see the point but once he did, the lessons really began.

Another instance happened with my senior student, Tom Corsin. He was partnered up with someone from a different school of arnis. His partner, in a good natured way, attempted to do change ups on him only to have his action countered immediately. Finally the guy said to him, *"You're a student of Dan's, aren't you."* Tom grinned at him. Counter the counter – very important.

This is why I say a key trap is to train solely for the perfect execution. I mix in training for the fail as part of my regimen. This sets me up to follow up from a failed technique. This is really valuable. That being said, students will always have personal preferences as to what they want to do so in that manner, I do allow some personal freedom of expression.

Being you were a fighter, I'm interested in your answer to this: There are those who believe fighters are born (with natural attributes, etc.,) and can't be made. What do you think?
Fighters can be made *if* they want to be made. Any person has certain natural attributes. As a skinny kid I had fast twitch muscles. Okay, I was quick. What I did not have was a large frame so I wasn't all that strong. I concentrated on developing my natural attributes while at the same time

developing my weak points so that they were stronger than when I began. You can always strengthen attributes a person does not naturally possess.

Skills can be taught, but heart (guts, courage) can't be. How do you approach building a student's heart for fighting?
That was a tough one for so many years but I finally found the key to developing someone's heart. In the words of Doctor Who, you "take the long way around." Let me provide the setting for my explanation. I will ask people at karate free-sparring seminars *"What is it that makes me qualified to teach this subject?"* I will get answers like I am a fighting champion or I am a high ranking black belt or that I am skilled or crafty and so on. Nobody has gotten the right answer yet. Why am I qualified? Simple. I was terrified of getting hit when I was a lower belt student, deathly afraid of it. I even failed my first karate belt test because my sparring was so bad. I had to overcome this fear so that I could go on to what I later accomplished. Let me repeat, I was afraid of getting hit. I worked for decades on how to develop an entry level of training so that anyone of any skill or attribute (or lack thereof) could successfully learn how to spar.

So, what is "the long way around?" If a person is afraid of getting hit then this is the first thing to take care of. How do I do it? By having a partner swing at them so slowly that the stick coming at them no longer represents danger but just a stick swimming at them through air. This gets someone familiar with the tool without the inherent danger normally associated with it. That handles the flinch.

Once the flinch response is neutralized, then I train the student in various ways of handling that slow-motion stick. Blocking, countering, dodging and so forth. These two steps will take as long as it takes. If the student begins to flinch, there is one thing I am sure of. The feeder (attacker) is going *too fast*. The defender is not the one making the mistake. The feeder is. So I make the feeder slow down.

Once the student is relatively comfortable with the above two steps, they begin to learn about sparring strategies and tactics. Then again they go through the process of being agonizingly slow so that again they do not flinch in the face of a sparring situation.

From here you do the same with any kind of contact with the stick to a meaty, not bony, area of the body. First you caress. Then you tap. Then they take a little harder hit than a tap until they can take an uncomfortable force to a meaty area without flinching too badly. The key point is to bring the student to the realization that the human body is tougher that they ever thought it was and they won't break upon first contact. All the while the student is training on the basics of the art. Familiarization with the tools and the actions will bring about a much braver student. In this way you can build heart in a student but it *is* the long way around.

Dan do you consider yourself to be a modernist or traditionalist? Or a blend of the two?
A blend of the two. I am a traditionalist when it comes to respect, manners, seniority and hierarchy. I have a very strong senior/junior ethic. I am a modernist in that I will not blindly stick to any one method if I find something that works better or helps me to teach better.

Do you think it's important for practitioners to adhere to the tradition of the system or look beyond their system of study to improve and adapt to modern times?
Once they have gotten everything from their base system, it can be time to move on. I did that with Modern Arnis. I stuck with Remy Presas for 21 years. Then he passed away. I could have stuck with what he taught me and continued to develop further skill in that or I could go outside the parent system to improve *my* art. The second option is more in line with how I personally develop. What I do now is what Bram Frank would call "Dan Arnis." The MA80 System Arnis/Eskrima is a tag for "Dan Arnis."

Bram and I - 2004 Seminar in Portland, Or.

Have the training methods you use continued to develop and change through your years of training and teaching? How have they evolved and where do you look for new and effective training methods to use?
The short answer to the first question is yes.

How my methods of training have evolved is if I see something missing in the training methods, I create one. A very simple one is the Blocking Form. It is an anyo (kata) consisting of 13 moves, variations of blocking actions so that the student becomes familiar with options. Another is what I call Block/Check-Counter-Counter. This is a beginning exercise in which the very beginning student is taught the rudiments of counter the counter. This is how I create them.

Another answer to the second part of your question of where do I look to find methods to use. YouTube or existing videos are great. There is a long range defanging drill that I hijacked directly from an Edgar Sulite video. I have hijacked training methods from videos of Mark Wiley and Antonio "Tatang" Ilustrisimo as well. Much like my development in my karate career, I will incorporate anything from anyone if it helps me or my students develop. A number of my innovations are, in fact, outright theft. LOL.

How do you approach teaching?
Basics, basics, basics and easy does it at the beginning. I match understanding with the physical movements.

Does your teaching focus more on explaining things clearly and concisely to the student or do you prefer them to work out a lot of their own understanding?
I never let a student figure it out. I spoon feed them like crazy. They will then have their own aha moments from their training and matching that with what I teach. For me, this is essential. For a student to progress rapidly and fully, they must understand what and why they are doing it. One of my long term students said to me the other day that one of the things she loves about how I teach is that I always have a reason for why I am teaching anything at any given moment. There is never a "do this and don't bother me with questions" sort of thing going on.

Some teachers believe a student should conform to the system and others believe it best to modify the system and their teachings to the students. What do you think is the best way?

It all depends on the mindset of the person. Some will remain true to the system and teach it the way they were taught. Others will modify and change. There is no right or wrong when you consider personal option. None. There is a difference between effective and ineffective, however.

In my school the curriculum will remain the same for any student training under me. That doesn't change. What changes is how I teach it to them. I've found in over the 50 years I have taught martial arts that not all students learn the same way. Some you can tell them what you want and they'll produce it. Others, when you talk to them you will see their eyes glaze over in a stupor. Some students are great mimics so all you need to do is to show them and off they go. Other students you might have to physically manipulate their arm or whatever for them to get it. You never know. So, I will, let's say, have 5-10 different ways of teaching a strike #1. The strike will be the same and in the same teaching order as proscribed in the curriculum but the manner in which I teach it will change from person to person, even if slightly.

In watching footage of Professor Remy teaching I can see some similarities with Guro Roland. Guro Roland would teach me something and not provide too much theory or explanations. I came to realise he wanted me to learn how to think/analyse.

You would find me to be quite a different type of teacher. I do not know about Guro Roland but I feel Prof. Remy was very intuitive with limited scientific vocabulary. His explanations were pretty rudimentary and not into the fine points. Martial analysis was not his strong point. That was left up to his senior students.

As one of the leading instructors in Modern Arnis who is dedicated to carrying on the teachings of your teacher, Professor Remy, how do you maintain quality and high standards amongst your instructors and students?

Hah! I rule with an iron hand in my school. You (a student) don't change a thing.

An important area fighters need to develop is good and effective footwork. How would you describe MA80 footwork?

The short answer is footwork is what enables you to use distancing, timing and alignment in your applications. To me, footwork needs to be simple. In order to work your footwork, there is something very simple to remember – bend your knees to be prepared to move. The biggest mistake in footwork is not being prepared to move to begin with. Footwork is important but preparation is even more important. If you are prepared to move, you can move right away. If you aren't prepared the first thing you will do when you see an opening is prepare to move and then move. Your movement will be the second thing you will do. You will lose a split second in your timing.

It appears Modern Arnis practitioners fighters prefer close range and are at a disadvantage at long range. How do you train students to effectively close the distance?

The majority of Modern Arnis players are at a disadvantage of not having competed extensively in karate matches. Karate matches taught me how to close the distance and the key to closing the distance starts in understanding range and distancing. From that point you need to know if you're blessed with explosive entry footwork or if you aren't. If you aren't then you need to work your way in to your opponent (firing a number of strikes as you advance) or develop a watertight defense and counter game. You asked earlier if I modify my teaching to go with the particular attributes of the student. This is where my teaching really follows the student's attributes.

Though Modern Arnis encompasses Largo, Medio and Corto ranges. Would you say Modern Arnis focuses primarily on medium and close range?

Remy Presas Modern Arnis is definitely medium and close range based. I try to maintain a balance between all three ranges. What I found out in my karate career was that any area you were deficient in was going to come back and bite you in the end. If a guy was a good kicker, you jammed his kicks and punched him. If he was a great puncher, you stayed away and kicked him. This was a basic tenet of how I applied myself in karate free-fighting. Become skilled at all ranges. If you look at my first book, you'll notice that I add in-fighting techniques and clinch techniques. While they are common today, they weren't common at all back in 1980. I apply the same attitude to the MA80 System.

You approach teaching the theoretical aspects of MA80 scientifically. How do you approach teaching the theory and ensuring students understand it?

I will explain the *why* of any action while I am teaching it. I am dead against a monkey see, monkey do teaching style. Mimicry has its place in following what your instructor is doing but I will always explain the why of any action as I teach it. I do not leave a student hanging. Understanding is a huge factor in becoming skilled in anything.

Regardless of students understanding the theory, the sign of understanding is being able to apply theory in applications against a non-compliant opponent. Would you agree?

Absolutely.

After learning the system and intensely physically training, do you think students see Modern Arnis as a concept approach and not technique approach to combat?

I can't/won't speak for anyone else but myself. At this point in my development, the MA80 System is totally a conceptual approach to combat.

For a Modern Arnis/MA80 practitioner to be able to be on a physical level with combat athletes, do you think they need to invest some time into strength and conditioning? After all fighters spar, skip and run regularly.

Sparring? Yes, to some extent. Combat athletes? Definitely. Ask Guro Doug Pierre what kind of shape he has to get into to win WEKAF world championships. He is the premier Modern Arnis player who competes in WEKAF competition. Actual combat? Not necessarily. Combat stick fighting is measured in seconds, not minutes or rounds. If you are doing sport stick fighting (WEKAF, Dog Brothers, FMA point fighting), then realize you are doing sport and not combat. Sport has rules of engagement no matter how rugged the sport is. Combat is going for the finish.

Guro Doug Pierre

In your eyes, what is the essence of Modern Arnis/MA80?
The essence of both systems are, to me, the Flow and counter the counter. Prof. Remy told me once, *"Danny, if you can counter the counter, you will not be beaten."*

What is the final goal of your teachings? To produce quality instructors?
Not really. My final goal is to make it easier for those who follow after me.

I have been gifted to be able to communicate principles simply so that the common man can understand and apply them. This was the one recurring comment in reviews of my first book, *American Freestyle Karate: A Guide To Sparring*. They could understand me. And that book changed lives.

Here is one such example. I received this via Facebook messenger the other day from Carlos Montalvo (Feb. 8, 2021): *"You do not have an idea how much you helped me with your first book, the way you explain things in such a logical way. I improved 100%."*

That is the goal of my teachings. I was a combination of inquisitive and driven so I searched out those who could provide me with answers to my questions and when I couldn't find anyone who could answer, I researched until I did find them. Then, I wrote books and shot videos based on my findings.

Can you share some of your most treasured/memorable times with Professor Remy both training and not training?

Training: One time he and I were doing the 6 count sumbrada drill and for some reason, I went into a disarm and disarmed him. I don't know if it was a muscle memory thing or what. I wouldn't normally do that to my senior. I thought that he was going to get mad and I was going to really have my ass handed to me. Instead, he said to me, *"Danny, that was very good but you forgot one thing. I am left handed. The cane was in my right hand."* He then put the cane in his left hand and took me to school with superb control. The lesson was that I was ready to take it to the next level and that there were gradations of excellence.

Personal: I remember sitting at an airport bar talking with him about some incident which happened when he was a kid. I told him that I wish I had a tape recorder with me so that I could get down stories from him when he was a kid and his development years. I told him they would make for a great book. He looked at me and said, *"Do you think people would be interested in that?"* At this point we were just two guys talking.

Reality Checks

Well, now that I am an arnis hotshot and I am flying solo, how do I keep myself from going off into Never Never Land with my stick work? There are several individuals who serve as reality checks for me. By the way, several of my reality checks are also influences in my MA80. I'll lay them out in order I videoed them. They are all equally important in my eyes. Following are edited transcripts of YouTube video shorts I did a while back.

Reality Check #1 – *Antonio "Tatang" Ilustrisimo*

Hi, Super Dan here. I'm going to present talking about what I call my reality checks.

My teacher, Remy Presas, passed away 21 years ago, and just like every other Modern Arnis, student, whether senior or junior, we've continued on our own personal paths. And without having him here, you know, I've made some subtle changes, and sometimes some big changes in what I do. But the thing that I look at is, since I don't have an instructor, presently, okay, what are my reality checks going to be? What are the things that are going to keep me in line? They're encompassed by five different people.

The first one, and the first one is Antonio "Tatang" Ilustrisimo. Now, this might come as a surprise to a number of people because Kalis   Ilustrisimo and Modern Arnis are very, very different from each other. Let me tell you how I got onto this and why.

Back in 2006, or thereabouts, I finally connected up with Mark Wiley, who is now a good buddy of mine, but he's also a very, very well-known Filipino Martial Arts author. We connected up in his hometown in Pennsylvania. And, you know, my flight comes in late, but man, we're just talking away and, you know, we pull out the sticks, we actually start sparring, and this is no pads this with control, etc. And he exposed a few holes in my in my fighting style. We stayed late in the night, we were talking, demonstrating, etc. And the fascinating thing was he the thing that got me was he "moved different-ly." Okay, if there's a movement pattern that I'm not familiar with, it's time to learn about that movement pattern.

He'd written a forward for the book *Secrets of Kalis Ilustrisimo* and in it he stated *"It was in Manila that I became a student of the late Grandmaster Antonio Ilustrisimo, and senior masters, Antonio Diego and Christopher Ricketts. It is a result of training with these men that I immediately felt saw a difference not only in the seriousness with which the seriousness with which they trained and view their art, but also in my skills compared to theirs. After a careful deliberation, I guess it assisted in my pursuit of other arts, and have been dedicated to the Ilustrisimo system ever since."*

Wow. That's an interesting declaration to make. So, after I read that, I started taking a look at Antonio Ilustrisimo and thanks to YouTube, I found a number of clips.

I'm gonna do a left turn at Albuquerque here really, really quickly. There's a phrase or there's a motto or a keynote statement that noted Japa-nese martial artist and historian, Kenji Tokitsu, had made. He said he had studied 50 different karate styles. But then he went to clarify, there's a big difference between studying the systems and training in the systems. He went on to say that he had only trained in actually a couple of systems, but he actually sat back and studied which means he carefully observed the differences and similarities of the various systems to come to certain viewpoints and hypotheses that he had. So, it is in this viewpoint that I started studying Antonio Ilustrisimo.

The thing that I noticed about him was that he was very, very combat ef-ficient. There was a phrase that Professor Remy would use all the time, *"No matter where you are, you're there already."* Well, with Ilustrisimo, no matter what position he was in, he was never out of position. And when I talk about efficiency I talked about, he cut right straight through, right straight to the meat of things. And he was simple, direct, precise, no wasted movement.

So, how was this my first reality check? I will consult the various videos, etc., that he does, and take a look at what I'm doing with other people and ask myself *"Am I getting too fancy? Am I getting a little bit unrealistic? Am I trying to chase a technique instead of doing what is there naturally?"*

I always go back to Antonio Ilustrisimo. In this respect, and whether I'm feeling my oats are not, I will refer to him as a reality check to see exactly what I'm doing with my art. So that is the first of my reality checks, Grandmaster Antonio Ilustrisimo of Kalis Ilustrisimo.

Reality Check #2 – *Manong Ted Buot*
Hi, Super Dan here. And this is the second installment of my own reality checks my five reality checks regarding Filipino martial arts. And in the first segment, I talked about Grandmaster Antonio illustrational. Now I want to talk about someone who I had actually trained with, and his name is Manong Ted Buot. And I'll start right off the bat. I trained with him very, very little. He lived in Detroit. I was in Gresham, Oregon, which is outside of Portland. And so to be perfectly honest, I only had a handful of lessons in the original style balintawak eskrima but the few lessons that I did have impacted my Modern Arnis so greatly that it changed pretty much everything that I do now.

How I met Manong Ted. Shortly after Professor Remy passed away in 2001, I started hearing about Ted from various sources. One of my good friends Jay Spiro, was a private student of his. Now, here's the interesting thing. The differences between Professor Remy and Manong Ted were very, very yin-yang. Professor Remy was quite outgoing. And Manong Ted was a quiet reserved gentleman. Professor Remy traveled all over the place and taught 1000s and 1000s of students. Manong Ted handpicked each one of the students and taught private lessons.

Manong Ted Buot and Dave Hatch

135

When we started training together here was another reality check for me. He had two things that were just uncanny. Number one was precision timing. And the other one was precision positioning. And although he moved totally different than Antonio Ilustrisimo, the simplicity, the directness, the precision, the no wasted movement, again, came to the surface.

And so when I look at what I am doing, I check myself. Am I am I wasting any action? Am I doing any added in applicable action? How can I cut down the amount of what I'm doing so that it becomes even more and more efficient?

And then the second thing is timing. In karate I have always been huge on timing. That was one of my main weapons. When I used to fight in karate tournaments my timing was impeccable. Well, it's the application of this same spot on timing to my stick work. I always refer back to my memories of Manong Ted because he didn't video. And like Professor Remy, who did tons and tons of videos.

He was in Professor Remy's words, *"No matter where you are, you're there already."* And so, thanks to Manong Ted, I take a look at timing, I take a look precision positioning. This is my second reality check. Although I trained very little with him, just a handful of hours; man, oh man, oh man, did he ever, ever, ever positively impact my Filipino martial arts!

Reality Check #3 – *Remy Presas*
Hi, Super Dan here. And this is the third installment of what I call my Filipino martial arts reality checks. Now I'm going to go with my teacher of 21 years, Remy Presas. He was the individual who turned me from being a karate jock into an actual martial artist. Professor Presas had it all. He had stick, he had knife, he had double stick, stick and knife, he had empty hand, he had joint locking, he had grappling - he had the whole ball of wax.

When I look at Professor Remy, in terms of being my reality check, one of the things I look at was that he always, always had an option. It didn't matter what kind of left turn at Albuquerque that you presented him with, he was always there with a counter. There was a phrase that he used that

136

became one of the four pillars of my own system, the MA80 System Arnis/Eskrima. That is *"If you can counter the counter, you will not be beaten."* I remember him telling me this many, many times. The first time this really sank in was when he started doing a variation of a six count drill where he would throw in actions that were not part of the standard drill and then bang, show you the counter for that. So, the thing that I got from him was there's always an option. No matter no matter where you are, no matter what you're doing, there's always an option.

Now, that was the first thing. The second thing was that the concept of the flow. And he was always impressing upon me, *"Danny, you must have the flow."* And so how do I describe the flow? Well, the flow is continuous, uninterrupted motion. And it doesn't matter whether the motion is being hindered. You just have a continuous motion. The example that I like to use the best is if you have a stream, you'll have rocks here and there. You know, a small rocks, big rocks, etc. in the stream. The water doesn't stop at the rock; it goes over it, it goes around, it goes under, it continues in motion.

So, when I look at everything that I do, whether it's empty hand martial arts, joint locking, throwing, stick work, stick and knife work, 1. I keep the flow in mind, am I doing this in a staccato fashion? Am I doing a series of stops starts? Or do I have continuous action?

And then the second thing that I look at is am I allowing myself to be stopped by somebody doing hindering action? Or do I automatically adjust and let it create my next move? This is, I think, is even more so important than the physical techniques that Professor me taught.

These are the aspects that have governed my martial arts life ever since I met him over 40 years ago. And so this is a brief discussion on how Professor Remy Presas is my third reality check. Because these are the things I look at. These are the things that I work on doing, making sure that I don't get caught up into being mentally and physically lazy. See you around. Super Dan, over and out.

Reality Check #4 – *Bobby Taboada*

Super Dan here and this is my fourth in a series of five installments on what I call my FMA reality checks. And now I want to get on to my fourth reality check. And this is Grandmaster Bobby Taboada. I know Bobby Taboada only peripherally. We first met in 1987. Peter Hill had brought me down to Phoenix, Arizona, to do a two day workshop on Modern Arnis. During the evening after the first seminar, he said there was somebody he wanted to introduce me to, Bobby Taboada.

Dieter Knuttel and Bobby Taboada

Bobby Taboada to water I had a student there and they gave me an exhibition of what I would find out later to be the grouping method of balintawak eskrima. The fascinating thing was these guys went full power, full out, full speed. And in about seven to 10 minutes, both of their sticks were shattered. I mean, I'm not talking about chipped. I'm not talking about dented. I'm talking shattered to where you could actually take one end of the stick just bend it. I was blown away. We went out later on that night and we chatted and he was very amiable, very nice fellow, and so forth. So I thought what I would do is I would I would look into what he did. I picked up a couple of his videotapes.

The fascinating thing, and this really spoke to me as a karate man, was his body dynamics, and this is where my fourth reality check comes in body dynamics. He used his entire body in the delivery of striking it, a lot of his motion was like boxing, you turn that body, wham. But he was doing this with a stick. I'm watching this and up until that point in time I was using my arm as the mode of delivery for the stick. But the thing was that I was *only* using my arm. Well, he was not only using his arm. He was delivering with stunning power and stunning speed.

It's interesting, because when you look at Grandmaster Bobby, especially the pictures of him back in those days, and he was built a lot like Prof. Remy. I mean, he was not this skinny little guy. I mean, this guy was massive, but he was using his body. One of the things that I've adopted as a motto is that *"I do not rely upon the hardness of the weapon to do the damage for me."* I use body dynamics, I use body action, I use rotation in everything I do with my with my stick work. And what that does is that A. it has increased my power in my strikes and B. it has brought about a lot more body coordination, which leads into everything else that I might be doing. This is the fourth reality check that I use for my own personal FMA. And we'll get on to the fifth one in the next segment.
There you go. Super Dan, over and out.

Reality Check #5 – *Leonard Trigg*
Hi, Super Dan here and this is the final installment of what I call my five reality checks. The fifth one epitomizes a viewpoint that I have about martial artists and that's for every one very well known or famous practitioner ,you have a number of them who are equally or better skilled, but they just aren't known all that much. Now, this individual I've known for over for 50 years. I have known him since he and I were both under belts. His name is Leonard Trigg, Professor Leonard Trigg. I'll give you just a tiny bit of background on, on Leonard.

I met him back in 1968-ish or something like that and he was the only person that I knew at the time who cross-trained in martial arts. He was doing karate at the Oregon Karate Association with me. He was also doing hung gar kung fu down in Portland Chinatown with Lee Fong. And now mind you, this is during a period of time where everybody is jealous of everybody else. If you did a different type of karate other than the one that you're doing, you're a traitor. If you did karate but you also did kung fu, you're being a traitor, and so forth. You know, cross training these days is very common. Back in the early, middle, and late 60s, it was not common at all but Leonard was ahead of his time.

Now besides karate and kung fu, he was an accomplished boxer and eskrimador. In fact, it's because of Professor Leonard Trigg that Ernesto Presas and Remy Presas were introduced into the Pacific Northwest. Now, aside from having trained with those two masters, he is also certified under Lucky Lucay-Lucay, and he's trained in the Ilustrisimo system as well as trained in the late Edgar Sulite's Lameco eskrima system. And these are just the ones that I know of. He's been to the Philippines many times. And those of you individuals who were at last year's Water and Steel (Kelly Worden's yearly camp), and got to take a class with him, you know he's a gentle giant…until he has a stick in his hands. When he has a stick in his hands, his body moves with *authority*.

What are the two reality checks as far as Professor Trigg goes? Well, number one, I just mentioned it moving with authority. This is having full confidence in everything that you're doing, and not having a back off or hesitation or whatever. Moving with authority. That's the first one. The second one, which is one that I aspire to; Leonard Trigg is probably one of the most humble masters that I have ever, ever met. And I've met lots. I've been in the martial arts for 56 years. There are a ton of people who I've met. Some had no humility at all. Some had false humility, you know, they played it up. But Professor Leonard Trigg? He's genuine. He's the real deal. He's respectful of others. He's respectful of other martial artists. I've never heard him say anything negative about anybody. Yet he can he carries himself with this tremendous authority. And when he moves, he moves with authority. And those two aspects put together are amazing.

So when I look at how I conduct myself in public, when I look at how I conduct myself with people, how close am I to genuinely emulating what I see in Professor Leonard Trigg? And if I get close, good, I'm doing a good job. Thus far, you know, I haven't had too many complaints. When I look at how do I present myself to others, am I moving with authority? At the same time am I contact friendly? Am I easily approachable?

Jackie Bradbury (Check out her Stick Chick blog) and I were talking one time and she had mentioned that one of the things that made me unique was how approachable I was. And that's a feather I would like to keep in my cap.

So, Leonard's my fifth reality check.

Just in in brief going over as a recap:

- "Tatang" Antonio Ilustrisimo. He's reality check as far as combat efficiency and simplicity.
- Manong Ted. He's my reality check regarding precision timing and precision positioning.
- Remy Presas. He's my reality check as far as the flow and available options.
- Bobby Taboada. Body dynamics - am I putting my body into everything? Am I utilizing my body with everything?
- Leonard Trigg. Do I move with authority that comes from within the inner confidence, but at the same time, am I as close to being humble as I can? Do I remain approachable?

I use those reality checks all the time. And to be perfectly honest, I feel my art is better for it. I feel my rapport with people is better for it.
There you go. Super Dan. Over and out.

Lakan Sampu

I am going to close this book of essays with something very special to me. What has come out of my 40+ year involvement with Modern Arnis? An acknowledgement to top all acknowledgement – the promotion to Lakan Sampu, 10th degree black belt in Modern Arnis, coming from the last surviving Presas brother, Roberto. Following is the published statement by the International Modern Arnis Federation, Philippines.

LAKAN SAMPU - 10TH DEGREE BLACK BELT
Official statement by International Modern Arnis Federation-Philippines (IMAFP) April 15, 2021

So it may be known, that, Grand Master Roberto A. Presas, Lakan Sampu (10th Degree) Modern Arnis and only survivor of the original 3 Presas brothers, by his leadership and wisdom decided that it is time to give recognition for the spreading of Modern Arnis in the USA, the country where his brother and founder of Modern Arnis, GM Remy A. Presas, Sr., taught for 25 years until his final days.

GM Roberto Presas wants to honor these 3 individuals (in no particular order):

Grandmaster & Datu KELLY WORDEN for making Modern Arnis his own in his Natural Spirit International (NSI), what GM Remy A. Presas always told his students to do and for his untiring efforts through seminars, camps and videos, acknowledging Modern Arnis as GM Remy Presas" contribution to the martial arts world.

Grandmaster DAN ANDERSON for his lifelong propagation of Modern Arnis through seminars around the world, his books and videos, where he unlocked the hidden secrets of GM Remy Presas by analyzing his movements, strategies and teachings and for finding his own approach to make Modern Arnis his own in his MA80.

Grand Master MoTT BRIAN ZAWILINSKI for his lifelong loyalty to the teachings and principles of GM Remy A. Presas through his worldwide seminars, camps and teachings as well as for the continuing effort to spread Modern Arnis in groups with different lineages and for making Modern Arnis his own in his "The art within your art" (TAWA).

GM Roberto Presas awards:
GM Datu Kelly S. Worden GM Dan Anderson GM MoTT Brian Zawilinski for their lifetime achievements to the rank of: "LAKAN SAMPU (10th Degree)" Grand Master of Modern Arnis.

This award is witnessed by:
GM Rene Tongson, Lakan Sampu (10th Degree), Modern Arnis
GM Samuel Bambit Dulay, Lakan Sampu (10th Degree), Modern Arnis
GM Datu Dieter Knüttel, Lakan Sampu (10th Degree), Modern Arnis

Their promotion to the rank & title is recognized by the International Modern Arnis Federation - Philippines (IMAFP), the homeland federation of Prof. Remy A. Presas, Sr. The award took effect on the date of signing. The certificates have been issued and signed by GM Roberto A. Presas and will be personally handed to the new Lakan Sampu's as soon as the pandemic restriction is cleared.

Mabuhay and congratulations from the Philippines!

(Sgd.) RENE R. TONGSON Chairman of the Board of Trustees
Attested: (Sgd.) GINALYN R. JADIA Dayang Pito (7th Degree) Secretary General

The following is from a video interview Dean Franco did with me and Brian Zawilinski on the promotion on FMA Discussion:

Dan Anderson:
The promotion to Lakan Sampu, I think, is very important for a couple of reasons. Number one is that the three individuals who received the promotion, myself, Brian Zawilinski and Kelly Worden, the first thing you notice is that none of us move the same. But we are representatives of the

Professor's art and we're spread across the country. We have all contributed. This is one very important thing. We've all contributed back to the art. I've done a number of seminars but the bulk of my contribution has been in my written and videoed materials.

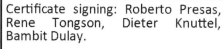

Certificate signing: Roberto Presas, Rene Tongson, Dieter Knuttel, Bambit Dulay.

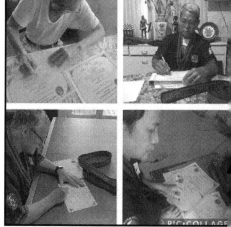

You know, Kelly, he's done a lot of military training, etc. constantly, constantly referring to the fact that Modern Arnis was that which gave him the key to unlock every other system that he did. You get Brian on the connections with the Philippines.

In the US, as far as Modern Arnis and IMAF Philippines, I think Brian's probably the most connected of all of all the guys here. So the first thing is that there's a recognition of how we have been forwarding the art. And yet Kelly's got his own expression, Brian's got his own expression, I've got my own expression, but it's pushing what the old man taught. Now that's the first thing.

Now, the second thing. And I I've been wondering how to say this delicately, there's no way I can say this delicately but we are the "next generation Remys." The "old man" passed in 2001. And as with any martial arts system; karate, taekwondo or whatever, when the senior (founder) passes, the senior students carry the ball. And so we are, in essence, the "next generation Remy Presas." I don't even like to say "students" because one of one of the things that I like about this, there's an acknowledgement of what we've done over the last 20 years.

It's very, very easy to remember how easily that the old man handled us, you know, he disarmed us quickly, joint locked quickly, or this or that. And it's too easy to get caught up into the memory of 20, 30, 40 years ago and forget the fact that we have progressed. You know, I've mentioned privately to Brian, *"Oh, geez, I wish the old man were alive now, because I'd like to scrimmage with him. And maybe he had hand me my ass but at the same time, it would be fun."*

Lastly, and I think the most important thing about the promotion. It is a recognized recognition from the homeland of the American legacy of Modern Arnis. It is not just, "Yes, Professor Remy spent the last 25 years here. Yes, it was the final development, the art." blah, blah, blah. It establishes that there is its own separate American legacy very much the same way that the German legacy was Dieter. There's a famous saying in karate – "The first five stripes (on your belt) are what you did to get them and the last five stripes are for what you've given back."

Okay, those of us have given back have received the acknowledgement from the homeland of an American legacy. We Americans already knew the American legacy, but this this establishes it from the home base, so to speak. To me, this is the importance. It's not a hierarchy thing. It's not a better than you thing, etc. I really I think it's a landmark. It's terrific. I'm honored to be, you know, to be one of the recipients, but it's a whole lot bigger than just me or just Kelly or just Brian, if we're talking Modern Arnis, America has its own legacy. And thank you for acknowledging the fact that we've done our part to continue, you know, take the art, make it our own and continue it.

Brian Zawilinski:

It's humbling and amazing. At the same time, we're still going strong. And I mean all of us, not just the three of us. I tip my hat to and I'm not just saying it because he's, he's sitting next to me (on the video screen). Dan Anderson doesn't need an introduction. Kelly Worden doesn't need an introduction. These guys have been studying longer than I've been alive. They're not just going quietly into the rocker. You know, we're very lucky to be part of the whole worldwide unity of modern arnis. And don't forget, when Professor passed there was some very dark years, the mud throwing, and just what an embarrassing time. But we got through it.

And here we are 20 years later. I've been to the Philippines twice. First time Dan was there as well. He's gone since then I went another time, just to be a part of this whole effort. Yes, we're all at different levels. It's okay. But how much of an effect this guy had on us. And to be able to connect with people from between the United States, East Coast and West Coast, there's 3000 miles. And Dan and I are either on the phone or shooting the text or giving each other hard time once or twice a week. It's got the whole country cornered. And then Dieter, in Germany, there's probably a week doesn't go by we don't touch base. And then you know, Bambit. And Rene. And when the late Cristino (Vasquez), God bless, was a lot. Steady contact globally over what? A martial art. That's pretty amazing.

You know, to be involved at this level, sometimes I still ask myself how the heck did this work out? But I think when you're at anything for any length of time, in this case, 40 years, you're going to learn. You're going to get the hang of it. And you get put in situations where you have an opportunity to give back. I don't believe in coincidences, I believe in hard work. You know, he (Prof. Remy) passed way too soon, he was shy of 65 years old. He's really, I mean, that guy kept getting better. If you watch the videos from the 80s, versus the 98 videos, he got a lot better. I could imagine what the next few years would have brought him. And, of course, all of us with him with him leading the way.

But I don't look at it in so much smaller pieces, I have a tendency to downplay awards and ranks and titles. And he gave me a title that was kind of unique along with the other six people when he was diagnosed in Germany, in late 2000. Which was amazing. But, you know, I was only 32 I'm not so sure I was able to truly appreciate the magnitude of that situation.

This is a whole different time now. 20 years past, we're traveling, we're growing, we're evolving, we're trying to get more of that many more people involved. And I think it speaks volumes of Modern Arnis world-wide, not just any particular group or level, that we're still doing it. And we've been through our share of ups and downs. But the art continues, and Dan said it best. *"The work continues."*

That's what the man wanted. He said, *"Do not let my art die."* And it's not. So you know, my whole thing is, is when things like this come along, it's very humbling. It's very appreciative to be, you know, recognized by the family twice. It's pretty cool. It is humbling. But if that tells me I'm heading in the right direction, but it also tells me, hey, don't stop. You're in a situation here where you can keep doing this and making connections and keep moving this thing forward. There's a little bit of responsibility with it, too. Yeah, you know, all in good positive en-ergy. So, I have a tendency to look at it in more broad strokes. But all is good. And it's humbling. It's, it's a hell of a journey. It ain't over. I'm just starting to get the hang of stuff.

Dan Anderson:
Let me add one thing to what Brian's mentioning is that I remember when I was promoted to 10th Dan in karate, and one of the first things I thought was *"Well, you know, it's kind of like a PhD."* So what do you do? What

do you do when you get a PhD? Now you go out and you do something with it. You go into your particular field and you discover the cure for cancer or the common cold or male pattern baldness, or whatever you do. But you don't get a PhD and then sit in your recliner, watching reruns of Oprah eating Bon-Bons in the afternoon. You take it, you run with it. And this is this is the same type of thing. It's like it's an acknowledgement/encouragement. "Thank you very much. What you've done (is) good so keep on keepin' on."

My "Peeps"

I dropped a comment earlier in this book a line about who I associate with, those individuals who share both martial ethics/culture and personal values as well. So, who are these mysterious people? There are several who I'll name here. There are actually a great number of people who I get along with and this list won't cover them all but here are the main ones.

Bruce Chiu, me, Bram Frank Brian Zawilinski, Roland Rivera

Brian Zawilinski - I met Brian at a seminar on the east coast but didn't really take much notice of him. It was the same when I attended ArnisFest in 2004. He was there but we didn't really connect. Then came the first Remy Presas Memorial Training Camp which was held the week before the 3rd World FMA Festival in 2006 in Tagatay, Philippines. The poor fellow was stuck with me as a roommate for two weeks. This was when I got to know him. What really impressed me about him was his taking what he experienced over what had been said. This had to do with Bram Frank. Brian had gotten some negative PR from others regarding Bram. After several days with Bram at the festival he said to me, "I don't know who this Bram that others are talking about but it ain't him." What he had done was take his own observation over the top of what others said. That, my friends, is integrity. Since that time Brian and I have become close friends. He is a man of integrity - what you see is what you get. No artifice, no tomfoolery, no BS. He has become one of my best friends, in martial arts and out.

Bram Frank, aka Brambo, Z'k. I met Bram back in 1994 and he is another example of what you see is what you get. Bram is the yin to my yang. I'm mostly a stick and empty hand guy while he is totally into the blade. He has taken what Remy Presas taught us and applied it to both the knife as well as the machete sized bolo. It was from him that I expanded my arnis play from stick to edged weapons. But there is more than just the technical side. Bram has got my back and I have his.

Bruce Chiu - I can't think about Bruce without smiling. I had heard of him for years and years but never met him until (at the time of this writing) a year ago. He and I hit if off like we'd been friends for decades. One interesting thing that I love about him is this statement - *"I am not a student of Filipino martial arts. I am a student of Remy Presas."* Beautiful honesty. Watching him move I vividly recall Prof. Remy moving with the same fluidity and grace. Good egg, that Bruce.

Loren Christensen - Loren was my first karate instructor and I still think of him as sensei. That speaks volumes. 'Nuff said.

Fred King - Freddy was the person who introduced me to the Professor. Fred was also a very close, personal friend of his as well. I can't speak enough about him.

Roland Rivera - I can't think about Roland with busting out into a big grin. I don't really know why but I have felt a kinship with Roland ever since I met him in Brevard in 2005.sort of thing. He is the one person I've met in Modern Arnis who doesn't care about the hierarchy or politics or any sort of thing. He just wants to train. Aside from his personality, this guy is mega-skilled. Any time I am around him, I feel better.

Chad Bailey - Here is another Bruce Chiu in his own way. Both he and Bruce exude a childlike joy when they are executing the flow of Modern Arnis. I watch him as a student and he reminds me of me when I am a student; taking voluminous notes and being a sponge, taking it all in.

Loren Christensen   Fred King (center)   Chad Bailey (right)

Kelly Worden - I have known Kelly since he wan an under belt. That's over 50 years. He and I have had a rocky relationship over the years but in the last ten years, we have been compadres. Kelly is his own man and follows his own code no matter who might disagree with him. That is integrity on his own path. I am glad that we are brothers. Salute.

Dieter Knuttel - Dieter and I got off to a slow start, thanks to my being a bit of a bonehead. I had gotten some bad PR on him and swallowed it hook, line and sinker. I taught a seminar in Germany in ~1994 and kept my distance. We both taught at the Modern Arnis Symposium in the early 2000s and I kept the same distance. In 2005, Dee Childress and I promoted the International Modern Arnis Seminar in Brevard, North Carolina. Dieter was one of the principal instructors. It wasn't until the end of the seminar when we connected. He was sitting at the computer looking at the screen of his wife and kids. He was melting in the chair. Ho! Dieter is a family man! Right then I figured I had not really looked at him, not really. From then on a beautiful friendship unfolded. One of the most impressive things about him is that we can have a disagreement about something (and we have had several good ones), discuss it like gentlemen and come away with a friendship that hasn't changed one bit except to getting stronger over the years..

Jaye Spiro - Smilin' Jaye. Jaye is one of the most positive people I have met. Love her to death.

Mark Wiley - Mark is not a Modern Arnis player, not really. He has trained with the Professor but then again, he has trained with a number of first rate instructors. Mark and I hit it off on first meeting. He is both an inspiration and a brother to me. Good fellow.

Jeff Burger - Coach Jeff! This guy reminds me of me when it comes to research! Jeff is so refreshing when it comes to martial arts. His perspective and analysis cuts to the bone AND he has a wicked sense of humor!

Michael Bates - I love his energy and passion for keeping the flame alive for Prof. Remy and Modern Arnis.

At this point you might be inclined to ask, *"Hey Dan, what about (insert your favorite Modern Arnis player here)? What's the deal? You didn't mention him/her!*

Well, this is a small list because I don't travel as much as I would like. I have directed my energy into writing, videoing and the continuation of my school (37 years at the time of this writing), not travelling all over the country doing seminars or frequenting the many halls off fame events.

These are the practitioners I hit it off very well with. There are many others who are not only good practitioners but wonderful people as well. I have listed my faves. That's all. If you or your instructor is not on this list, don't read any more into it other than I am not in constant contact with them on a daily or weekly basis. That's all.

After Word

July 31, 2021 - Good morning [west coast time]. I am in a terrific mood so I have a different kind of rant today, a very positive one.

Let me preframe this with my last visit with Prof Remy Presas before he passed away. He said something I thought was odd at the time. He reached over, touched my arm and said, *"Danny, get involved."* My internal thought was *"I was never NOT involved."* All I said was *"Yes, sir."* and we continued on with the visit. I found out later that he thought that I had retired.

You see, in 1997, my daughter Charlie was born and I stayed home to raise her instead of being a "seminar rat" (an affectionate term, by the way) and travelling all around the country were over.

Fast forward 20 years and the world is in the grip of the pandemic. I received an email from Jose telling me how the school he attended for Modern Arnis lessons had closed (temporarily) because of it and how he redoubled his efforts to train by learning the anyos I had posted up on YouTube to continue his training. We had a video chat this morning and he told me how he trained 6 days a week on the anyos at varying speeds and rhythms. I melted in the chair.

I was a world class karate player when I met Prof. Remy but there was a huge piece of the martial arts pie that I didn't have. Remy Presas opened the door for me to move forward from being a karate player to martial artist.

Since his passing, I have been very INVOLVED in spreading his art in the best way that I am suited for - via written and videoed materials. I am not an organization man. That is not my direction. I leave that to Dieter Knuttel and others as they have that as a strong point. I teach and thank goodness for Y2K technology, my ability to reach others is now worldwide.

My strong points? One of my strong points comes from my karate days is that I am a very analytical student. I pick apart the pieces of any action to see how the technique works. I did that a lot with Modern Arnis. I remember learning the double action abaniko in a private class and Fred King saying to me, *"You are learning this by osmosis."* Not really. I trained my observational skills to a high level as well as training my body to be ambidextrous so that whatever Prof. Remy taught, I picked it up rather quickly and accurately. Loren Christensen refers to me as a "natural learner."

Another or my strong points is that I can take any martial arts material and make it easily learnable. If y'all remember, I wrote the first comprehensive book on karate free-fighting, American Freestyle Karate - A Guide To Sparring. One of the key features of that book (as well as any that I have written subsequently) is that I communicate so that anyone of any aptitude or skill set can duplicate and apply the materials. My Modern Arnis materials follow that to the point where someone like Jose, who I have never met, can take what I do to face the pandemic head on and enhance his skills.

Thank you, Prof. Remy, for giving me this art. Yes, GIVING. *"Yes, sir. I am involved."* *bow*

Well, there you go. What started out to be a small project and turned into a book.

Okay, it's time for me to get off the computer and get back to training. There are sticks to swing. I hope you enjoyed the read.

DA

About The Author

Dan Anderson has been a major figure in the world of USA martial arts for decades. He began training in karate in 1966 and went on to become a regional, national and international karate champion. Anderson authored the first groundbreaking work on karate fighting, *American Freestyle Karate - A Guide To Sparring* and is hailed as one of the leaders in the evolution of American Karate.

He met Prof. Remy A. Presas in 1979 and this marked another journey, this time into the world of Filipino Martial Arts. He trained with Presas from 1980 until his passing in 2001 achieving 6th degree black belt and Senior Master status. Dan Anderson is a founding member of the Worldwide Family of Modern Arnis.

During his career, Anderson has written and produced 28 books and ~100 martial arts videos being one of the most prolific authors of martial arts materials in the United States.

During his half century career in martial arts, he now holds four 10th Dan ratings:

- Karate (Allen Steen & J. Pat Burleson)
- Modern Arnis (Roberto Presas - Presas Legacy, Roberto Presas - International Modern Arnis Federation of The Philippines).

He is the founder of two distinct martial arts programs: American Freestyle Karate and the MA80 System Arnis/Eskrima.

He has compiled *The Modern Arnis Archival Series* - a collection of books and videos that fully detail the art of Modern Arnis and its many facets. This can be found on his book and video website www-superdanonlinelibrary.com.

Anderson continues to teach at his school, Anderson Martial Arts, in Gresham, Oregon. You can contact him at dannyleeanderson@hotmail.com.

The Super Dan Online Library

www.superdanonlinelibrary.com

Karate Books

American Freestyle Karate: A Guide To Sparring

Fighting Tactics & Strategies

Beyond Kick & Punch

The Anatomy of Motion

The American Freestyle Karate Black Belt Manual

American Freestyle Karate - The Master Text

Super Dan - A Martial Arts Memoir

The Gathering Chronicles - The Quest For Kudan

Itosu's Legacy

The Hidden Link - Kata & Free Fighting

The Super Dan Method of Free-Fighting

Conversations With Super Dan

Arnis/Eskrima Books

De-Fanging The Snake - A Guide To Modern Arnis Disarms

Advanced Modern Arnis

Mano y Mano

Trankada

Modern Arnis - The Art Within Your Art

Espada y Daga

Labanan Solo

Filipino Martial Arts

Advancing Your Martial Arts

Modern Arnis For The New Millennium

Shintai Kyousei Jutsu

Steel Meets Flesh

Modern Arnis - The Martial Art of Remy Presas

Modern Arnis Mano y Mano

The North American Legacy of Remy Presas

Karate DVDs

The American Freestyle Karate Curriculum

The Anderson Martial Arts Karate Curriculum

How To Teach Free-sparring To ANYBODY!

Itosu's Legacy

Motion Application Bunkai - Nai-hanchi Shodan

Positional Set Up

Point! & Match! World Championship Winning Moves

Super Dan Method of Free-Fighting

Super Dan Super Seminar - Deceptive Footwork

Super Dan Super Seminar - Germany Seminars

Arnis/Eskrima DVDs

Combat Principles of Filipino Martial Arts

Arnis Combatives Simplified

Motion Application Breakdowns of Modern Arnis Anyo/Kata

How Balintawak Eskrima Influenced My Modern Arnis

The "Big If" -Self-Defense Against A Knife

The Roots of Modern Arnis - The Blade

The Classical Styles of Modern Arnis

2021 Modern Arnis Tribute Camp

De-Fanging The Snake

Dos Manos - Two-Handed Weapons of Modern Arnis

The Essence of Tapi-Tapi

Flow Disruption

The Heart of Modern Arnis - The Flow

Flowing Like Water

Fast Track Arnis Training Program Vols. 1-5

Super Dan Super Seminar - Germany 2019

Laying The Foundation

LvR - A Right Hander's Guide To Training The Left Hand

Mano a Mano

Modern Arnis Cane & Empty Hand Joint Locks

The Path Alone Signature Throws & Takedowns of Modern Arnis

Sumbrada Shadowing

Mini-Ebooks

The Art of Joint Locking - Finger Locks

The Art of Joint Locking - Wrist Locks

The Art of Joint Locks - Elbow & Shoulder Locks

Filipino Martial Arts - Cane Locking & Choking Techniques

Karate Sweeps & Takedowns

The Physics of Throwing

Modern Arnis - The Art of Tapi-Tapi

The Art of Effective Defense

Trapping Hands Simplified

Super Seminar Downloads

Flow Disruption - Connecticut Modern Arnis Camp 2021 (1 video)

The Hidden Bladework of Modern Arnis (1 video)

International Modern Arnis Seminars (3 videos)

Presas Brothers Arnis Seminars (2 videos)

Portland Filipino Martial Arts Festivals (5 videos)

Stick & Steel - Impact & Edged Weapons Seminars (9 videos)

Upcoming Titles

Free-Sparring Trifecta With Super Dan

Free-Fighting Footwork Hacks For Karate & Arnis

The Complete Super Dan Book of Kata - Execution & Applications

MA80 System Arnis/Eskrima White-Black Belt Curriculum

Made in the USA
Middletown, DE
15 October 2022